The 100 Greatest Jews
in Sports

Mike Epstein and Ron Blomberg offer another way to ask Abbott and Castello's classic question as a pickoff attempt brings two Jewish first basemen together. This might be the only photo ever taken of two Jewish professional ballplayers competing. (Photo courtesy of the California Angels, by Sam Spina.)

The 100 Greatest Jews in Sports

Ranked According to Achievement

B. P. Robert Stephen Silverman

The Scarecrow Press, Inc.
Lanham, Maryland, and Oxford
2003

SCARECROW PRESS, INC.

Published in the United States of America
by Scarecrow Press, Inc.
A wholly owned subsidary of
The Rowman & Littlefield Publishing Group, Inc.
4501 Forbes Boulevard, Suite 200, Lanham, Maryland 20706
www.scarecrowpress.com

PO Box 317
Oxford
OX2 9RU, UK

British Library Cataloguing in Publication Information Available

Library of Congress Cataloging-in-Publication Data

Silverman, B. P. Robert Stephen
  The 100 greatest Jews in sports : ranked according to achievement /
B. P. Robert Stephen Silverman.
     p. cm.
  Includes index.
  ISBN 0-8108-4775-2 (pbk. : alk. paper)
  1. Jewish athletes—Biography.   2. Jewish athletes—Rating of.
I. Title: One hundred greatest Jews in sports.   II. Title.
GV697.A1 S516 2003
796'.089'9240922–dc21   2003009603

Dedication

With apologies to Abbott and Costello, these are the names of the players on my all-time team. Shown are the poodles Bogie and his father Pompo on second and third base; the spitz Stroupie is at shortstop; the cocker spaniel Honey is behind the plate, at catcher; and the collie Buddy is in right field. My mother, Clara Lavenstein Silverman, the exquisite champion golfer of her country club, appears with the collie, who is in left. Lady Pompie—a grandniece of Buddy and my partner during my prime—and the poodle Cappuccino are in center field. Continuing clockwise are Buddy and I, celebrating our undergraduate degree; my sole surviving family member, the bichon frise Wendy, "My Girl," who literally shares my chair as I write this, is on the mound. Lady Pompie, Cappuccino, and I appear together. Finally, there is my father, Abraham George Silverman, a Clark Gable look-a-like and legendary second baseman for whom later-day Hall of Famer Nellie Fox might very well have been known as "an Al Silverman, but without the power" had he stuck with baseball. The answer to "Who's on First?" apparently then has to be Blackie—a dog of many ethnic origins from my early childhood—who is the only member of my lifetime family not shown on this montage. Each of them has a place in my heart because of my parents, whose fierce desire to protect animals from people was a product of their constant remembrance of the Holocaust, not as survivors but as proud Jews. My mother's last words were "We have always been Jewish. Never let anyone take our Jewish religion away from us."

(Photos Courtesy of B. P. Robert Stephen Silverman.)

Contents

Cover Photo Credits and Captions   viii

Acknowledgments   ix

Preface   xi

1   The Scope and Criteria of the Rankings   1

2   The Quantitative Ranking Criteria   7

3   The All-Time Ranking of Great Jewish Athletes   15

4   All-Time Rankings by Era   139

5   Unsung Jewish Athletes   143

6   Jewish Sports Team Executives   149

7   The Jewish Sports Following   157

8   Milestones in Jewish Sports History   167

9   The Jewish Sports History IQ Test   173

Epilogue   181

Index   183

About the Author   187

Cover Photo Credits and Captions

Top: Jay Fiedler makes it look easy as he completes a quick 10-yard pass to Randy Moss against the Washington Redskins. (Photo courtesy of the Minnesota Vikings.)

Left: In 1956, Hank Greenberg became the first Jewish member of the National Baseball Hall of Fame. (Photo courtesy of the Detroit Tigers.)

Center: It is staggering to imagine how great he could have been, but Sandy Koufax's Hall of Fame plaque suggests that he was still the greatest pitcher ever. (Photo courtesy of the Los Angeles Dodgers.)

Right: This rare minor league photograph of Shawn Green captures the current superstar before his explosive power was discovered. Although he stands 6'4", Green was initially thought to be more of a high-average contact hitter than a power threat. (Photo courtesy of the Toronto Blue Jays.)

Acknowledgments

This book would not have been possible without benevolence of the Jewish athletes who provided me with exclusive quotes; public relations practitioners who provided me with photographs of them; and readers of my previous book, *The Jewish Athletes' Hall of Fame*, who wrote me letters through the publisher from as far away as South Africa advising me of the Jewish athletes I missed. But the inspiration for writing it came from the six million Jewish martyrs and every victim of isolated anti-Semitism.

The appearance of decreasing anti-Semitism toward most Jews almost everywhere has a potentially extraordinary consequence. It increases vulnerability of a selected Jewish person somewhere. A comparative scarcity of them now makes anti-Semites not seem as obvious and memories of The Holocaust not as vivid. History has shown what can happen in an immoral country that is rampant with virulent anti-Semitism. Even in a moral civilization, a Jewish person becomes vulnerable when a public figure makes anti-Semitic remarks; or when an anti-Semite is misplaced in a position of public trust. Anti-Semites can abuse their power by manipulating systems to exclude one Jew, when excluding one Jewish person is all the evil that can be done; or by turning entire systems against a selected Jew, to stalk, slander, or sabotage that Jewish person, in a worst-case scenario, when that can be done. No Jew can afford to ever forget the six million Jewish martyrs and the victims of isolated anti-Semitism; nor can the rest of society.

B. P. Robert Stephen Silverman, Ph.D.

Preface

Current baseball superstar Shawn Green is projected to place sixth in the rankings—just ahead of legendary boxer Benny Leonard, but behind football lineman Ron Mix. Golfer Amy Alcott ranks at number 20, some sixteen places in front of hockey's Mathieu Schneider and fifty above baseball's Mike Epstein.

This book definitively ranks the greatest Jewish American athletes of modern times from all major sports against one another according to achievement. Yet it is written for nonsports fans, people who see parallels in sports with mundane events in their own lives. The book is light, but it touches on serious issues of concern to every Jewish person while respecting the demands for accuracy of those who take sports seriously. It also presents answers to questions that I have raised to the most famous of Jewish athletes for more than three decades. I am invariably asked about one of those questions more often than any other.

The question came up in a 2003 bestseller about a legendary Jewish athlete. That author's hundred-word interview of me cited my 1989 book, which introduced an *All-Time Ranking of Great Jewish Athletes* in revisiting my question—a question about a possible connection that I had discovered between one of the most extraordinary of events in Jewish history and a simultaneously sudden emergence of that athlete from an inconsistent to a historically unparalleled performer that very night. This book explains that possible connection and presents a compelling case for induction into the National Baseball Hall of Fame of a Jewish pitcher under the precedents that were established for induction of similarly excluded African Americans.

Chapter 1

The Scope and Criteria of the Rankings

If such a vast number of Jewish athletes had not attained greatness in so many major sports over the past one hundred years, it would not require a complex methodology to rank them according to achievement. Every decade has seen someone different emerge as the greatest Jewish athlete.

Boxer Abe Attell held the distinction as the greatest Jewish athlete at the turn of the twentieth century and turned over that mantle to fellow boxer Benny Leonard in the teens. Then came football's Benny Friedman in the twenties, baseball's Hank Greenberg in the thirties, and football's Sid Luckman in the forties. Basketball's Dolph Schayes took over in the fifties, followed by baseball's Sandy Koufax and Ken Holtzman in the sixties and seventies, respectively. Golfer Amy Alcott emerged as the top Jewish athlete in the eighties. In the nineties, Alcott passed the title to football's Harris Barton.

Already, the first decade of the twenty-first century belongs to baseball's Shawn Green. Just comparing those eleven great Jewish athletes introduces a maze of extraordinarily difficult decisions. To meaningfully rank the greatest Jewish athletes in all major sports from those eleven decades against each other requires a limited scope and quantitative criteria. It also entails inevitable value judgments. Deciding whether to exclude Jewish athletes who converted to other religions became extremely difficult. Without distinguishing between Jewish athletes who married within the faith and those who never set foot in a synagogue, I decided

1

that excluding converts out of the religion would have created an intellectually dishonest double standard.

Therefore, I knowingly included baseball's Lou Boudreau and Bo Belinsky, basketball's Nancy Lieberman, boxing's Mike Rossman, and golf's Corey Pavin despite their reported conversions out of Judaism. In making that value judgment, I reflected on an interview that I later read in which a great Jewish athlete was asked whether he had celebrated a bar mitzvah and whether his wife was Jewish. The athlete showed justifiable signs of intense discomfort in contending that he still planned to take Hebrew lessons and that his wife eventually would become a Jew.

An easy value judgment I made was to exclude participants in any activities that are cruel to animals. Bullfighting puts a positive spin on torture in an obvious way, and more than two thousand racing horses are put to death each year because of equally grotesque resultant track injuries behind the scenes. There is no sport in hurting animals.

However, I had no litmus test for political correctness. In the early 1990s, many newspapers reported that debate was briefly raised in Israel over whether to drop tennis star Amos Mansdorf from that country's Davis Cup team for his alleged speculation that he might have considered competing in the 1936 Berlin Olympics had he been born fifty years earlier. I would have included Mansdorf anyway, but he primarily competed outside the United States.

I limited the scope of my All-Time Ranking of Great Jewish Athletes (chapter 3) to athletes who competed primarily in the United States since 1900. That enabled me to include 1960s Israeli soccer player Roby Young for his career with the New York Cosmos and 1920s British boxer Ted "Kid" Lewis, who got his fights in the United States; and to exclude Angelica Roseanu, Robert Cohen, Angela Buxton, Alphonse Halimi, Jody Scheckter, Martin Jaite, Mansdorf, and possibly David Beckham, if unconfirmed reports he is Jewish are true.

Roseanu emerged as the top woman table tennis player in the world in the 1930s. In 1954, Cohen decisioned Chamren Songkitrat to become bantamweight champion of the world, only to lose it the following year when Mario D'Agata knocked him out. Buxton reached the finals of the 1956 Wimbledon championship and shared a win in the doubles tennis competition before a wrist injury ended her career. The following year, Halimi scored a technical knockout over D'Agata with a Mogen David on his trunks to capture the bantamweight crown and held it two years.

In the 1970s, Scheckter gained prominence out of South Africa as a race car driver. Jaite, an Argentinean, defeated German superstar Boris Becker in 1986. Beckham is currently the best soccer player in Europe.

Current baseball catcher Mike Lieberthal made the 1999 National League All-Star Team and hit .300 that year with 31 home runs while winning a gold glove as best at defense of his position as well. In 2000, Lieberthal's home run total dipped to 15 in slightly fewer than 400 plate appearances, and he managed only 121 at bats the following year because of injuries. Lieberthal would warrant a projected place in the All-Time Ranking of Great Jewish Athletes but is excluded because of a Jewish heritage that extends only to his father.

With the exceptions of 1970s auto racer Peter Revson and tennis star Tom Okker, I excluded all athletes whose only Jewish heritage came from their fathers. The late Revson expressed gratitude in being included in my Jewish Athletes' Hall of Fame, and Okker reportedly supported many Jewish causes. The most accomplished excluded athlete with Jewish heritage was 1970s baseball Hall of Fame pitcher Jim Palmer, whose adopted father has been reported and was described on a World Series telecast of a game that he pitched against Sandy Koufax as Jewish.

For knocking out Nazi Germany's sports idol Max Schmeling with a Star of David on his trunks, I included boxing champion Max Baer despite his having only an alleged strain of Jewish heritage. That was a no-brainer.

I did take, though, a scholarly approach toward ensuring reliability and validity by identifying the most common categories of statistics in which the highest-paid athletes in all sports had excelled. In each sport, it quickly became evident that athletes are collectively paid more for excelling in certain combinations of specific performance categories, so I assigned numeric values to reflect those.

That provided a proportional representation of the most important individual accomplishments in sports. By applying those numbers to the records of selected athletes, I ranked them against each other and asked selected experts of each sport to do the same—but with only general guidance and no specific criteria whatsoever. After repeatedly modifying categories and values, I achieved consistency between the applications of my numeric values and the experts' subjective rankings.

I compared points compiled by the highest-rated athletes of one sport against athletes of similar and substantially different standings in other sports. Then I further modified categories and values until I finally arrived at an apparent consistency in ranking athletes of different sports against each other. To ensure reliability and validity, I repeatedly tested and revised criteria until the rankings consistently had a meaningful order.

It took extraordinary means to quantitatively find similarity in such dissimilar records as those of Barney Ross in boxing, Harry Newman in football, and Issac Berger in weightlifting with those of Dick Savitt in tennis, Buddy Myer in baseball, and Max Zaslofsky in basketball.

I imputed the point totals of five Jewish superstars—Ken Holtzman, Dick Savitt, Benny Friedman, Buddy Myer, and Max Zaslofsky—to project what they likely would have accomplished had they not been forced into premature retirement or simply denied recognition they deserved, by apparent discrimination, and ranked them accordingly.

Absent symptoms of discrimination, I still would have imputed their point totals to compensate for statistical anomalies that resulted in lower rankings than they deserved. As an analogy, if Roger Maris had been Jewish, the 40 points his achievements warrant would include 14 points for induction in the National Baseball Hall of Fame—even though he was never admitted—because of the gross inequity of his inexplicable exclusion. To account for a statistical anomaly that proved too advantageous, I adjusted the point total of Abe Attell downward.

I projected point totals to reflect what is likely to be accomplished by such current athletes as Shawn Green, Jay Fiedler, Mathieu Schneider, Gabe Kapler, Jason Marquis, and Scott Schoeneweis. I did the same to reflect an anticipated Hall of Fame induction for Harris Barton.

The differing number of Olympic medals awarded in various sports was first raised by an observation of 1964 Olympic swimming silver medalist Marilyn Ramenofsky. In a 1973 letter to me, she stated, "Medals are not given equally among all the sports; for example, there are many more medals given in swimming than in gymnastics." If I had simply awarded points for the number and types of Olympic medals won, as distinct from the number of Olympiads any number of a given medal was won, the great Jewish swimmer Mark Spitz would have been ranked on the basis of 67 points. Primarily for one monumental month in 1972 in a less popular sport, he would have then exceeded the 65 points that reflect Sid Luckman's legendary twelve-year career as one of football's greatest quarterbacks.

There are only eight categories in which male gymnasts compete for gold in comparison to twice that many for male swimmers, who have thirteen individual events—ranging from five lengths of freestyle swimming to two lengths each of backstroke, breaststroke, butterfly, and medley—in addition to three relay events that award swimmers individually.

Only one gold medal is awarded to each member of the winning basketball team and the champion of each weight class in boxing. I simulated the disparity under a hypothetical scenario that Teofilo Stevenson, the superheavyweight Cuban boxer, had been Jewish. He won gold medals in the 1972 Munich, 1976 Montreal, and 1980 Moscow Olympics with victories that included horrifying knockouts cited as among the most one-sided victories in Olympic history. If points had been awarded for the number of medals won, that would have left Stevenson, had he been Jewish, with 21 points, less than one-third as many points as Spitz—who captured two gold, one silver, and one bronze medal in the 1968 Mexico City Olympics before winning an amazing seven gold medals in the 1972 Olympics at Munich. Spitz was the greatest swimmer ever, but Stevenson was the best Olympian of a generation.

A meaningful comparison of the number of medals won could only be drawn if boxing had offered opportunities to win multiple gold medals in each weight class—perhaps for matches of three, six, nine, twelve, and fifteen rounds in the same manner that swimming awards individual gold medals for 50-meters, 100-meters, 200-meters, 400-meters, and 1,500 meters in just freestyle events alone.

Therefore, I awarded points for the number of Olympiads in which an athlete won any number of gold; silver, but no gold; or bronze, but no gold or silver medals. Stevenson's achievement of winning gold medals in three Olympiads warranted 21 points, compared to the 14 points reflecting Spitz's seven gold medals as a swimmer in two.

Chapter 2

The Quantitative Ranking Criteria

Points	Baseball
14	Selection to National Baseball Hall of Fame
12	Each year with:

1. 450 at bats and a .400 batting average;
2. 56 or more home runs;
3. 170 or more runs batted in;
4. 30 or more pitching wins.

10   Each year with:

1. 450 at bats and a .380 to .399 batting average;
2. 40 to 55 home runs and a .340 to .379 batting average;
3. 25 to 29 wins and a 2.09 or lower earned run average;
4. 375 or more pitching strikeouts;
5. 82 or more games saved.

4   Each year with:

1. 25 to 39 home runs and a .340 to .379 batting average;
2. 40 to 55 home runs and a .300 to .339 batting average;
3. 25 to 29 wins and a 2.10 to 3.50 earned run average;
4. 19 to 24 wins and a 2.09 or lower earned run average;
5. 300 to 374 strikeouts;
6. 70 to 81 games saved.

3   Each:
         1. perfect game pitched;
         2. game with 4 home runs;
         3. year with 450 at bats and a .340 to .379 batting average with less than 25 home runs;
         4. year with 25 to 39 home runs and a .300 to .339 batting average;
         5. year with 40 to 55 home runs and a .270 to .299 batting average;
         6. year with 25 wins and a 3.51 or higher earned run average;
         7. year with 19 to 24 wins and a 2.10 to 3.09 earned run average;
         8. year with 55 to 69 saves.
2   Each:
         1. All-Star selection;
         2. imperfect no-hitter pitched;
         3. World Series pitching win;
         4. year with 450 at bats and a .300 to .339 batting average with fewer than 25 home runs;
         5. year with 19 to 24 wins and a 3.10 or higher earned run average;
         6. year with 15 to 18 wins with a 3.09 or lower earned run average;
         7. year with 30 to 39 home runs and a .270 to .299 batting average;
         8. year with 40 to 55 home runs and a .250 to .269 batting average;
         9. year with 40 to 54 games saved.
1   Each year with:
         1. 250 to 449 at bats and a .300 to .339 batting average with fewer than 25 home runs;
         2. 15 to 18 wins with a 3.10 or higher earned run average;
         3. 25 to 39 games saved.

Sample Application of Ranking Criteria

Hank Greenberg's record in Major League Baseball merits a total of 80 points:

14	Selection to the National Baseball Hall of Fame
24	12 points each for 170 runs batted in during 1935 and 58 home runs in 1938
10	10 points for 41 home runs and a .340 batting average in 1940
4	4 points for 40 home runs and a .337 batting average in 1937
12	3 points each for 26 home runs and a .339 batting average in 1934; 36 home runs and a .328 batting average in 1935; 33 home runs and a .312 batting average in 1939; and 44 home runs and a .277 batting average in 1946
<u>16</u>	2 points for each of eight All-Star team selections
80	

Points	**Football**
14	Selection to Pro Football Hall of Fame
6	Each year averaging at least 3 touchdown runs or passes for every game scheduled during the season
5	Each year averaging at least 100 yards rushing or 6 pass receptions for every game scheduled for the season, or 1 interception for every other game scheduled
4	Each All-Pro and College All-America team selection
3	Each Championship Game (or Super Bowl) touchdown run or pass
2	Each year starting in more than half of the regular season games on the winner of the championship game (or Super Bowl)
1	Drafted in first round

Sample Application of Ranking Criteria

Ron Mix's record in professional football merits a total of 51 points:

14	Selection to the Pro Football Hall of Fame
36	4 points for each of nine times he was named All Pro
<u>1</u>	Drafted in first round
51	

Points	Basketball
14	Member of the Basketball Hall of Fame
3	Each professional year averaging a total of 40 or more points, rebounds, and assists per game
2	Each professional year averaging a total of 30 to 39 points, rebounds, and assists per game
1	Each All-Star team and College All-America selection; each professional year averaging a total of 20 to 29 points, rebounds, and assists per game

Sample Application of Ranking Criteria

Dolph Schayes's record in professional basketball merits a total of 57 points:

14	Member of the Basketball Hall of Fame
9	3 points in each of three seasons for averaging totals of 40 or more points, rebounds, and assists
20	2 points for each of ten seasons of averaging a total of 30 to 39 points, rebounds, and assists
<u>14</u>	1 point for averaging a total of 20 to 29 points, rebounds, and assists in each of two seasons and twelve All-Star team selections
57	

Points	Bowling
3	Member of Professional Bowling Association Hall of Fame
1	Each year with the leading average game score

Points	Boxing
21	Ranked first in Nat Fleischer's universally recognized and widely reported All-Time Ranking
14	Ranked second in Nat Fleischer's All-Time Ranking
7	Ranked 3 through 10 of all time by Nat Fleischer
6	Each year as undisputed heavyweight champion
5	Each year as undisputed champion of lighter weight class
4	Each year as an ununified heavyweight champion
3	Each year as an ununified champion of a lighter weight class

Sample Application of Ranking Criteria

Benny Leonard's record in professional boxing merits a total of 49 points:

14	14 points for being ranked among All-Time Lightweights by Nat Fleischer
<u>35</u>	5 points for each of seven years as undisputed World Lightweight Champion
49	

Points	**Golf**
14	Each major championship:
	1. U.S. Open
	2. PGA Open
	3. Masters
	4. British Open
	5. U.S. Women's Open
7	Among Top Ten All-Time Leading Money Winner

Points	**Tennis**
12	Each major singles championship: (1) U.S. Open; (2) Wimbledon; (3) French Open; (4) Australian Open
5	Top 10 ranking

Sample Application of Ranking Criteria

Dick Savitt's record in professional tennis merits a total of 41 points:

24	12 points for winning the Wimbledon Singles Championship once and another 12 points under the premise that he would have won it again had he not been forced into premature retirement by discrimination
12	12 points for winning the Australian Singles Championship
<u>5</u>	5 points for his Top 20 ranking.
41	

Points	**Hockey**
14	Selection to Hockey Hall of Fame
8	Total of 2,000 goals and assists over career

6	Career game average as goalie of 2.00 or less goals against
6	Total of 1,000 to 1,999 goals and assists over career
4	Each All-Star team selection
3	Each year with a plus-or-minus average of +25 or more
1	Each full year on a Stanley Cup champion
1	Each year with a plus-or-minus average of +10 to +24

Points	**Olympics**
7	Number of Olympiads with gold medal(s) won
3	Number of Olympiads with silver but no gold medal(s) won
1	Number of Olympiads with bronze but no gold or silver medal(s)

Points	**Soccer**
1	Each All-America or All-Star team selection
1	Each year starting in more than half of the regular season games or the winner of the final championship game

Points	**Auto Racing**
7	Each major championship: (1) Indianapolis 500; (2) IndyCar; (3) Winston Cup; (4) Daytona 500; (5) World Grand Prix
3	Each National Hot Rod Association championship

More Sample Applications of Ranking Criteria

Sid Luckman's record in professional football merits a total 65 points:

12	Selection to Football Hall of Fame
10	5 points for the two years (1943 and 1947) that he averaged at least 3 touchdown passes per game
4	4 points for each of 1943, when he intercepted 4 passes in eight games playing defense in addition to quarterback
14	2 points for each of his 7 championship game touchdown passes

4	One point each for playing more than half the scheduled games of the 1940, 1941, 1943, and 1946 Chicago Bear championship teams
<u>21</u>	Three points each for six All-Pro and one College All-America team selections
65	

Sandy Koufax's record in Major League Baseball merits a total of 78 points:

14	Selection to National Baseball Hall of Fame
40	10 points for his 382 strikeouts in 1965 and 10 points for each of his three seasons with 25 to 29 wins and an earned run average of 2.09 or lower
6	3 points for a perfect game; 3 points for his 1964 record of 19 games won and a 1.74 earned run average
<u>18</u>	2 points for each of six All-Star team selections; and 2 points for each of three imperfect no-hitters
78	

Sid Luckman's 65 points placed him third behind Hank Greenberg (left) and Sandy Koufax on the All-Time Ranking of Great Jewish Athletes. A reasonable case could be made to rank each of them as high or higher than any athlete, regardless of religion. That proved to be the case in applications of my methodology to various Gentile athletes.

This Hank Greenberg ace is not enough to hold on to his three-year reign as the Dewar's Sports Celebrity Tennis Tournament Championship in 1974. Three decades earlier, Hank Greenberg earned his distinction as the greatest Jewish athlete. In a 1973 letter to me from his son, Stephen Greenberg wrote, "My father was always proud of his heritage, but resented being called the greatest Jewish slugger of all time when in fact he may have been the greatest slugger of all time." (Photo courtesy of Schenley Affiliated Brands Corporation.)

Chapter 3

The All-Time Ranking of Great Jewish Athletes

Bracketed numbers next to each name represent the athlete's points compiled against the author's quantitative ranking criteria.

Rank	Points
1	Hank Greenberg [80]
2	Sandy Koufax [78]
3	Sid Luckman [65]
4	Dolph Schayes [57]
5	Ron Mix [51]
6	Shawn Green [50, projected]
7	Benny Leonard [49]
8	Ken Holtzman [46, projected]
9	Dick Savitt [41, projected]
10	Benny Friedman [39, projected]
11	Lou Boudreau [37]
12	Buddy Myer [34, projected]
13	Barney Ross [32]
14	Nat Holman [30]
15	Harris Barton [28, projected]
16	Battling Levinsky [27]
17	Al Rosen [25]
18	Marshall Goldberg [22]
19	Ted "Kid" Lewis [22]
20	Amy Alcott [21]
21	Corey Pavin [21]
22	Maxie Rosenbloom [20]

23	Lyle Alzado [20]
24	Abe Attell [19, adjusted]
25	Max Zaslofsky [18, projected]
26	Harry Newman [17]
27	Nancy Lieberman [17]
28	Louis "Kid" Kaplan [17]
29	Jackie Fields [17]
30	Rudy LaRusso [16]
31	Ed Newman [15]
32	Mark Spitz [14]
33	Issac Berger [13]
34	Kenny Bernstein [12]
35	Randy Grossman [11]
36	Mathieu Schneider [11, projected]
37	Harry Danning [10]
38	Sid Gordon [10]
39	Henry Wittenberg [10]
40	Mark Roth [9]
41	Erskine Mayer [8]
42	Neal Walk [7]
43	Lew Tendler [7]
44	Steve Stone [7]
45	Art Heyman [7]
46	Jay Fiedler [7, projected]
47	Lou Gordon [6]
48	Max Baer [6]
49	Harold Solomon [5]
50	Steve Tannen [5]
51	Brian Gottfried [5]
52	Brad Gilbert [5]
53	Julie Heldman [5]
54	Aaron Krickstein [5]
55	Eliot Teltscher [5]
56	Elise Burgin [5]
57	Jay Berger [5]
58	Tom Okker [5]
59	Larry Sherry [4]
60	Goody Rosen [4]
61	Sonny Hertzberg [4]

62	Mark Clear [4]
63	Lenny Rosenbluth [4]
64	Brad Edelman [4]
65	Richie Scheinblum [4]
66	Jason Marquis [4, projected]
67	Gabe Kapler [4, projected]
68	Mike Rossman [3]
69	Roby Young [3]
70	Mike Epstein [3]
71	Mitch Gaylord [3]
72	Barry Asher [3]
73	Marshall Holman [3]
74	Marilyn Ramenofsky [3]
75	Barry Latman [2]
76	Mike Hartman [2]
77	John Frank [2]
78	Paul Weintraub [2]
79	Art Shamsky [2]
80	Morrie Arnovich [2]
81	Elliott Maddox [2]
82	Ron Blomberg [2]
83	Shep Messing [2]
84	Bo Belinsky [2]
85	Scott Schoeneweis [2, projected]
86	Ernie Grunfeld [1]
87	Albert Schwartz [1]
88	Donald Cohan [1]
89	Brent Novoselsky [0]
90	Andy Cohen [0]
91	Brad Ausmus [0]
92	Danny Schayes [0]
93	Scott Radinsky [0]
94	Al Levine [0]
95	Ronnie Stern [0]
96	Bruce Mesner [0]
97	Joel Kramer [0]
98	Ross Brooks [0]
99	Alan Veingrad [0]
100	Peter Revson [0]

ON THE CORRECT CONNOTATION OF 0 POINTS

A score of 0 points appearing next to an athlete's name does not suggest a lack of success—at least not in the context of the All-Time Ranking of Great Jewish Athletes. It merely indicates that none of the quantitative criteria could be objectively applied to draw a meaningful comparison with achievements of the vast majority. To appreciate the fine line between an achievement that qualifies for points and a compilation of 0 points with an ability that is commensurate or superior, consider how the ranking criteria would apply to comparisons of two pairs of Gentile boxers: Pete Redemacher with Zora Folley and Teofilo Stevenson with Jerry Quarry.

Neither Folley nor Quarry came up through amateur boxing at the year of an Olympiad or won the world heavyweight championship during their distinguished careers as primary contenders for the crown. Therefore, neither ever realized achievements that would have warranted any ranking points. Redemacher's achievement of winning a superheavyweight gold medal for the United States at the 1956 Olympic games in Melbourne, if he had been Jewish, would be worth 7 ranking points. If Jewish, Stevenson would have warranted 21 ranking points for doing the same for Cuba at the 1972 Munich, 1976 Montreal, and 1980 Moscow Olympic games. However, Redemacher was knocked out in his second professional fight by Folley, and Quarry would likely have done the same to Stevenson if the Cuban fighter had turned pro. If they had been Jewish, Zora Folley and Jerry Quarry might have nevertheless earned spots in the All-Time Ranking of Great Jewish Athletes with 0 points beside their names; but ranked well ahead, if they had been Jewish, would have been Teofilo Stevenson and Pete Redemacher with 21 and 7 points, respectively. That would have been consistent with my objective to rank athletes according to achievement.

Hank Greenberg (left), with a player who exemplified his same grace and style, Joe DiMaggio. (Photo courtesy of Schenley Affiliated Brands Corporation.)

NUMBER 1
HANK GREENBERG [80]

Hank Greenberg had a consistency that would later be the trademarks of Williams and DiMaggio with the power that would emanate from Mantle and McGwire. With the sweet swing of a latter-day Maris and Bonds, he had the clutch timing of a Sosa and Mays. He was closer to Babe Ruth in ability than were those who would better Ruth's records with a livelier ball. It is hard to imagine how many home runs Ruth or Greenberg might have hit had they played in 1998—or how Greenberg would have hit had he not missed the five prime years of his career and batted ahead of Lou Gehrig as did Ruth, because Greenberg missed four full seasons at his absolute peak to combat service during World War II and another complete year because of a broken wrist.

Current conditions have changed the number of home runs that modern players hit, but Hank Greenberg's power has never been equaled from the right-side of the plate. (Photo courtesy of the Detroit Tigers.)

Greenberg retired with a career total of 331 home runs at a ratio of 1 homer every 15.69 times at bat—an extraordinary accomplishment when compared to the ratio of 1 home run every 16.38 times at bat that Hank Aaron maintained for his Major League Baseball career-record 755 home runs. During the three prime years preceding his military service, Greenberg averaged a home run every 12.34 at bats.

If Greenberg had maintained that pace during the five prime years he missed, his career ratio would be reduced from the 1 homer every 15.69 times at bat that he maintained to 1 home run every 14.35 times at bat. If afforded the same opportunity of 12,364 at bats that Aaron had, it then could be imputed that Greenberg would have hit 861 home runs over the course of a full career—a career not interrupted by four years of military service and another year lost to injury.

Given the livelier ball used in the current era by expansion diluted pitching staffs and admissions in 2002 by two former Most Valuable Players that they had used performance-enhancing steroids, records compiled by Greenberg take on added significance.

The September 12, 1935, issue of *Sporting News* contained a cartoon of Greenberg together with a circular-pacing and large-nosed man, hunched over and saying, "Oy Yoy-Oy Yoy." Some thirty-five years later, in its October 3, 1970 issue, an article in that newspaper recalled Greenberg's greatness as a baseball player in this way: "The Jews have long since proved that, even if they don't like it, they can take it." Decades after his career ended, Greenberg is slighted whenever an all-time team is named. Lou Gehrig is invariably selected for first base. The emphasis placed on Greenberg's religion might still distract from his play.

The record that Greenberg compiled was phenomenal—58 home runs in 1938; 63 doubles in 1934; 183 and 170 runs batted in during the 1937 and 1935 seasons. He had batting averages of .340 in 1940, .339 in 1934, and .337 in 1938; and more than 200 hits in 1934, 1935, and 1937. It took only three years before Barry Bonds would break the record that Mark McGwire set in 1998 of 70 home runs. But approximately three-and-a-half decades would pass between the times that Roger Maris eclipsed the single-season home run record of Babe Ruth and when his record was eventually surpassed. During those seventy-four years, no player came closer to breaking Ruth's single-season record than did Greenberg in 1938—some sixty years, ironically, before that threshold of home runs would become reachable.

In 1938, Greenberg needed only 2 homers to reach sixty with five games to play. Suddenly, pitchers stopped putting the ball over the plate. Greenberg's only choice was to swing off balance at pitches way out of the strike zone or take the walks and lose whatever chance he had of hitting another home run.

It was during the last game of that 1938 season when Greenberg uttered his often-quoted concession line. When darkness forced umpire George Moriarty to call a premature end in the sixth inning, he said, "Sorry, Hank, but this is as far as I can go." Then Greenberg replied, "That's all right, George, this is as far as I can go, too."

The October 3, 1970, *Sporting News* linked Greenberg's four years of military service to the purge of Jews in German-controlled countries and indicated that the thirty-year-old Greenberg could have avoided service either because of flat feet or a law permitting discharge of soldiers who were twenty-eight or older. Greenberg paid a heavy price for defending his country and fighting for Jews who were being oppressed.

In a 1973 letter to me, Hank Greenberg reflected briefly on his career: "During my baseball career, I do not recall experiencing any prejudice; I do not consider name calling racial prejudice." In his edited book, *Hank Greenberg: The Story of My Life*, Ira Berkow captures Greenberg's recollections of his thoughts about Adolf Hitler during the course of a game.

On June 11, 1973, I received a long letter from Hank Greenberg's son, then a minor league first baseman. These were the thoughts that Stephen Greenberg shared with me:

As a full colonel fighting Hitler on General Douglas MacArthur's immediate staff during World War II, my father played handball on several occasions with Hank Greenberg. "Getting to know Hank as I did," he said, "convinced me that he had an internal resolution to stay in the service, even though it meant foregoing enormous earnings and, of course, risking his life." Some three decades would pass before my mother, shown here with my father, would be briefly introduced to Hank Greenberg after hearing so much about him over the years. "It was immediately evident that all of the things I had heard about him being such a gracious and nice person were completely true," she recalled. (Photos courtesy of Abraham George [Al] Silverman.)

After slugging 44 home runs in 1946, Greenberg was waived out of the American League to the Pittsburgh Pirates, where he closed out his career as the first $100,000 athlete. (Photo courtesy of the Pittsburgh Pirates.)

My father was always proud of his heritage, but resented being called the greatest Jewish slugger of all time when in fact he may have been the greatest slugger of all time regardless of background. . . . I am pleased guys like Ken Holtzman, Mike Epstein, Richie Scheinblum, and Ron Blomberg have achieved success in the Major Leagues. But, I have never felt that their careers have any effect or direct relationship to mine. My father's career really has no bearing on mine. [However,] I do feel a kind of closeness to other Jewish ballplayers that is difficult to explain.

On the jacket of Ira Berkow's edited memoirs of Hank Greenberg is a quote from National Baseball Hall of Famer Ralph Kiner regarding Greenberg's quest to be commissioner of Major League

At Yale, Stephen Greenberg followed in the footsteps of not only his legendary father by playing baseball but former President George H. Bush as the first baseman and captain of the Yale University baseball team. (Photo courtesy of Yale University.)

Baseball. After an unsuccessful attempt at a Major League Baseball career, the younger Greenberg almost achieved the only thing that his legendary father had wanted to do but could not. As a Yale graduate and Berkley attorney, Stephen Greenberg was a logical candidate. Then when Fay Vincent became commissioner of Major League Baseball, Greenberg assumed the vacated post. As deputy commissioner and chief operating officer, Stephen Greenberg appeared a good bet to someday assume the position his father had always coveted for himself. However, being a hand-picked deputy of Fay Vincent would soon become more of a liability than an asset. Vincent alienated team owners by exerting more independent authority than desired by the team owners who paid his salary. When Vincent quit, team owners would not authorize his successor to make any independent decisions. Soon, Greenberg resigned as well.

Despite a respectable minor league career in such cities as Denver, Stephen Greenberg lacked the home run power expected of a first baseman and never advanced to the Major Leagues as a player. (Photo courtesy of Stephen Greenberg.)

The Legendary Record of Hank Greenberg

Year	Pos	AB	Hits	2B's	HR	RBI	BA
Career	1B/OF	5,193	1,628	379	331	1,276	.313
(1933–1941 and 1945–1947: Tigers and Pirates)							
Season Bests			203	63	58	183	.340
Best Five Years							
1934		593	201	63	26	139	.339
1935		619	203	46	36	170	.328
1937		594	200	49	40	183	.337
1938		556	175	23	58	146	.315
1940		587	195	50	41	150	.340
Composite		587	195	46	40	158	.332

Greenberg's 58 Home Runs in 1938 by Team Game

HR	Game	HR	Game	HR	Game
1	1	21	66	40	109
2	3	22	66	41	110
3	7	23	72	42	112
4	14	24	74	43	114
5	16	25	74	44	119
6	18	26	75	45	120
7	20	27	80	46	122
8	25	28	81	47	132
9	30	29	85	48	133
10	30	30	87	49	133
11	32	31	87	50	135
12	35	32	88	51	139
13	37	33	88	52	140
14	50	34	90	53	140
15	54	35	90	54	143
16	55	36	91	55	146
17	59	37	92	56	146
18	60	38	99	57	150
19	61	39	109	58	150
20	61				

NUMBER 2
SANDY KOUFAX [78]

It might have been fitting for Sandy Koufax's eventual Hall of Fame plaque to have been presented to him by Nazi hunter Simon Wiesenthal. It may have just been a coincidence, but the reason for Koufax's sudden emergence could have more to do with the pride instilled by Wiesenthal in his Jewish heritage than even Koufax realizes.

On May 23, 1960, Israeli Prime Minister Ben-Gurion announced that Wiesenthal had captured the despicable Adolf Eichmann—a Nazi Holocaust kingpin. That night, a potentially great Jewish baseball pitcher with control problems and a career-losing record pitched a one-hit shutout; and, from that point on, the Jewish pitcher dominated Major League Baseball as no pitcher ever had—hurling four no-hitters, including one perfect game; winning three times as many games as he would lose; and striking out more than one batter per inning over the next six years. From that point on, Sandy Koufax exhibited the self-confidence he lacked in order to achieve the greatness that had been predicted for him.

Ironically, a game that Koufax did not pitch may have been his most important. He sat out the opening game of the 1965 baseball World Series in observance of Yom Kippur, and Jewish people in all walks of life suddenly had a larger-than-life precedent not to work on the High Holy Days. It had been thirty years since Hank Greenberg had set that precedent. The public needed reminding. I reached Koufax in East Holden, Maine, in 1973 and asked whether he had felt an obligation because of his prominence to exert influence on public opinion in support of Jewish issues. "My personal feelings have always remained private, and I would prefer to keep it that way," he replied.

Sandy Koufax was arguably the greatest baseball pitcher ever, past or present—from Cy Young and Walter Johnson preceding him at the turn of the century, and two decades later to Nolan

The lightning speed of Sandy Koufax makes his left hand appear to be a blur. (Photos courtesy of the Los Angeles Dodgers.)

Ryan, Roger Clemens, Greg Maddox, Pedro Martinez, and Randy Johnson.

Koufax threw so hard that when he mastered control of his pitches, he was virtually unhittable. His fastball had so much velocity that it carried an aura of fear and anticipation—the fear of sudden death, by the sickening thought of a batter being struck by a ball traveling at that speed, and the anticipation of witnessing a perfect game or no-hitter. The movement of his curveball was compared to a ball dropping off a table at lightning speed.

Koufax retired from baseball because of arthritis at only thirty years old. He had pitched just eleven years, and the first half of that was squandered because of infrequent use by his manager, Walt Alston. In *Koufax*, his autobiography published with Ed Linn by Viking Press, 1966, the former southpaw presented a 1956 column from the *Daily News* by Dick Young. The column raised questions regarding why Alston only reluctantly pitched Koufax and yanked him at the first sign of trouble.

The infrequent use of Koufax caused him to have control problems, and Alston cited this resultant lack of control as the reason for infrequently pitching him. As a consequence, the development of Koufax was curtailed. On a Bob Costas radio show, *Coast to Coast*, anti-Semitism was speculated by a guest as a reason why Koufax was pitched so sporadically.

His last name evolved into the adjective most frequently used when attempting to succinctly describe the highest possible level of performance by a pitcher. (Photo courtesy of the Los Angeles Dodgers.)

When Koufax finally was made part of the starting rotation, he had to pitch in constant pain because of arthritis. It is difficult to imagine how great he could have been.

The Legendary Record of Sandy Koufax

Innings	Strikeouts	Wins	Losses	Earned Run Average
		Career Record (1955–1966: Dodgers)		
2,324	2,396	165	87	2.76
		Season Bests		
	382	27		1.73

Comparative Records during Koufax's Career

Record from 1955 through May 22, 1960

Wins	Losses
28	31

Performance on May 23, 1960 (When Eichmann Was Arrested): One-Hit Shutout

IP	H	R	ER	W	SO	ERA
9	1	0	0	6	10	0.00

Record after Eichmann Was Arrested

Wins	Losses
119	43

Best Five Years

	IP	SO	W	L	ERA
1962	184	216	14	7	2.54
1963	311	306	25	5	1.88
1964	223	223	19	5	1.74
1965	336	382	26	8	2.04
1966	322	317	27	9	1.73
Composite					
	275	289	22	7	1.95

Koufax's No-Hitters

Koufax's First No-Hitter, June 30, 1962

New York Mets	*At bats*	*Hits*
Ashburn lf	3	0
Kanehl 3b	4	0
Mantilla 2b	3	0
Thomas 1b	2	0
Cook rf	3	0
Hickman cf	3	0
Chacon ss	2	0
Cannizzaro c	3	0
R. Miller p	0	0
Davisult p	2	0
Woodling ph	0	0
Christopher ph	0	0
New York Mets	000 000 000—0	
Los Angeles Dodgers	400 000 10x—5	

Koufax's Second No-Hitter, May 11, 1963

San Francisco Giants	*At bats*	*Hits*
Kuenn lf	4	0
F. Alou rf	3	0
Mays cf	3	0
Cepeda 1b	3	0
Bailey c	2	0
Davenport 3b	3	0
Amalfitano 2b	3	0
Pagan ss	3	0
Marichal p	2	0
Pregenzer p	0	0
McCovey ph	0	0
San Francisco Giants	000 000 000—0	
Los Angeles Dodgers	001 003 04x—8	

Koufax's Third No-Hitter, June 4, 1964

Philadelphia Phillies	*At bats*	*Hits*
Rojas cf	3	0
Callison rf	3	0
Allen 3b	2	0
Cater lf	3	0
Triandos c	3	0
Sievers 1b	3	0
Taylor 2b	3	0

Amaro ss	3	0
Short p	2	0
Roebuck p	0	0
Culp p	0	0
Wine ph	1	0
Los Angeles Dodgers	000 000 300—3	
Philadelphia Phillies	000 000 000—0	

Koufax's Fourth No-Hitter, September 10, 1965 (perfect game)

Chicago Cubs	*At bats*	*Hits*
Young cf	3	0
Beckert 2b	3	0
Williams rf	3	0
Santo 3b	3	0
Banks 1b	3	0
Browne lf	3	0
Krug c	3	0
Kessinger ss	2	0
Amalfitano ph	1	0
Hendley p	2	0
Kuenn ph	1	0
Chicago Cubs	000 000 000—0	
Los Angeles Dodgers	000 001 00x—1	

NUMBER 3
SID LUCKMAN [65]

Even by modern standards, the greatest football quarterback of all time may be Sid Luckman. In 1943, while also playing defense—as incredible as that might seem today—Luckman compiled a higher single-season percentage of touchdown passes to passes thrown than did any of the other great quarterbacks in football history who would follow him—Sammy Baugh, Johnny Unitas, Joe Montana, Terry Bradshaw, John Elway, Brett Farve, Sonny Jurgenson, Dan Marino, Roger Staubach, and Joe Namath included. Luckman's 28 touchdown passes in only 202 attempts could be considered equivalent to throwing 70 touchdown passes now. Current quarterbacks may throw that many passes in five or six games, and their teams now play twice as many games.

Former Bears' owner George Halas revolutionized a run-oriented game by designing the T-formation. Then, the game

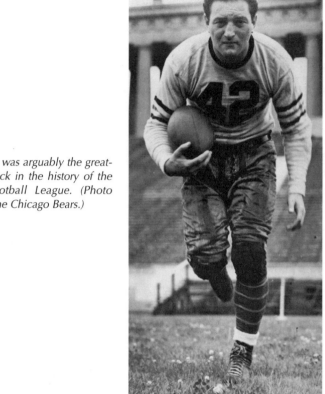

Sid Luckman was arguably the greatest quarterback in the history of the National Football League. (Photo courtesy of the Chicago Bears.)

was structured around the single-wing formation, in which the center snaps the ball to a left halfback or fullback—generally for a power sweep behind the blocking of a quarterback and right halfback. Frequently, the initial running back would lateral to a teammate running behind. In a single-wing formation such as this, it's unbalanced to the right. The right halfback lines up behind the right end, and the blocking quarterback might line up behind the right guard such that either the fullback or left halfback are in position to receive a snap from the center—who is situated closer to the left end rather than at the middle of the line.

Sid Luckman was the first to implement the T-formation; today all teams use it. In the T-formation, the center hands the ball under his legs to the quarterback, who might fake a handoff to a halfback or fullback and drop back to pass in search of a receiver. After lettering three years both as a halfback in football and shortstop in baseball at Columbia University, he was drafted by the Pittsburgh Steelers, who immediately traded his rights in one of the worst sports blunders ever—to Chicago. Luckman led the Bears to championships in 1940, 1941, and 1943; losing in 1942 when the Washington Redskins rebounded from a 1940 Luckman-directed 73–0 trouncing to post a 14–6 defeat on the Jewish quarterback.

Luckman was voted All-National Football League quarterback seven straight seasons and Most Valuable Player in 1943, when he passed for 28 touchdowns in a season that was approximately half as long as those expanded through modern scheduling. He retired in 1950, and it took fifteen years for the Pro Football Hall of Fame to admit him.

The Chicago Bears's 1946 *Press Book* contains this passage about Luckman: "In the matter of touchdown passes and yardage gained by passes, Luckman is tops by himself. . . . Sid is the slickest ball handler and smartest signal caller in the history of the T formation." In a 1973 letter to me, then Pro Football Hall of Fame librarian Jim Campbell provided a breakdown of Luckman's career statistics.

In 1947, Luckman averaged almost nine yards per carry running the ball. No current quarterback ever plays defense. Luckman punted thirty-four times in 1943; and over his entire career, he intercepted 14 passes for 293 yards and 1 touchdown.

Current quarterbacks have game plans more dependent on the pass and new rules that enable them to complete more passes. Yet few ever equal the 28 touchdown passes that Luckman threw in 1943 and the 24 he threw in 1947 in twice as many games.

In a June 30, 1973, letter to me, Luckman answered some difficult questions that I had posed to him in this frank way:

No, I was not aware of any special following from Jewish fans or any other ethnic group.

As for exercising influence as a spokesman about Jewish or any issues, I am not, nor ever was an orator, and always left this to political figures or heads of government.

My talents were strictly athletic, and whenever called upon to speak publicly it was always in relation to my sport and the people connected with it. As athletes, I don't think we're qualified, or well enough informed to voice opinions on the grave issues you mentioned.

Using me as a point of reference, Luckman elaborated:

You are a young man and must remember my playing days were before, during, and just after World War II. Before the "Bill of Rights," "Women's Lib," and the rest that might be making it more

The Legendary Record of Sid Luckman

Regular Season Record in Eight-Game Seasons
(1939–1950: Chicago Bears)

Year	Attempt	Completed	Intercepted	Yards	TDs
1939	51	23	3	636	5
1940	105	48	9	941	6
1941	119	68	6	1,181	9
1942	105	57	13	1,023	10
1943	202	110	12	2,194	28
1944	143	71	11	1,018	11
1945	217	117	10	1,725	14
1946	229	110	16	1,826	17
1947	323	176	31	2,712	24
1948	163	89	14	1,047	13
1949	50	22	3	200	1
1950	37	13	2	180	1
Totals	1,744	904	130	14,683	139

Championship Game Record

Year	Opponent	Score	Attempts	Completed	Yards	TDs
1940	Redskins	73–0 win	4	3	88	1
1941	Giants	37–9 win	12	9	160	0
1942	Redskins	14–6 loss	12	5	2	0
1943	Redskins	41–21 win	26	15	276	5
1946	Giants	24–14 win	22	9	144	1
Totals			76	41	670	7

difficult now for a Jewish or black athlete, or one of Polish, Irish, or German extraction.

But, during my time, the fans were all for the game and applauded and appreciated a bright or clever maneuver and booed an error or stupid play.

Luckman reflected on his era by recalling that "an individual was judged by his ability to perform, his sportsmanship—good or bad—and his talent in his particular field."

Sid Luckman gained recognition as the best athlete in the world during the worst period ever in world history. (Photo courtesy of the Chicago Bears.)

NUMBER 4
DOLPH SCHAYES [57]

Decades after Dolph Schayes retired from basketball, the best skills of certain elite forwards inevitably warrant a comparison with a particular part of his game. Kevin McHale possessed a comparable level of offensive post moves, equivalent passing skills were exhibited by Larry Bird, and Karl Malone had a similar level of power rebounding. Keven Garnett possesses his versatility. No single player, however, has ever mastered every aspect of the forward position indisputably better than the ambidextrous Hall of Famer with a patented two-handed set shot, Dolph Schayes.

Three times, he averaged more than 40 total points, rebounds, and assists per game; for another ten years, he totaled more than 30. After the 1948–1949 season, Schayes was voted Rookie of the Year. When he retired, no player had been elected to more All Na-

Dolph Schayes arguably remains the greatest forward ever to grace a basketball court. Excerpt of letter from Schayes to me in 1973: "There aren't enough Jews in sports, but Jewish athletes do perform a valuable public relations service for American Jews. Obviously, American Jews take pride in accomplishments of successful Jewish athletes, not only on a national level but down the line in high school. Public opinion is influenced by attention getters—whether they be athletes, clergymen, or politicians—speaking intelligently on any issue. Prejudice, for the most part, has left the American sports scene at all levels. In fact, most teams are on the lookout for Jewish athletes." (Photo courtesy of Dolph Schayes.)

tional Basketball Association Teams or had ever scored as many points—an achievement that reflected breaking the record of Minneapolis Laker George Mikan, who until Bill Russell and Wilt Chamberlain arrived had been considered the most dominant big man ever to play the game.

With durability comparable to a later-day Cal Ripkin in baseball, Schayes went nearly ten years without missing a game. At six feet eight inches, he often played with his back to the basket, but he could drive to the hole with the speed of a small forward or shoot from long distance with either hand. Schayes made first team All-Star in the 1951–1952, 1952–1953, 1954–1955, 1956–1957, and 1957–1957 campaigns; and on the second team in the 1949–1950, 1950–1951, 1955–1956, 1958–1959, 1959–1960, 1960–1961, and 1961–1962 seasons. For coaching the Philadelphia 76ers to the 1965–1966 title, Schayes was named NBA Coach of the Year. He was bypassed by the National Basketball Hall of Fame until 1972.

NUMBER 5
RON MIX [51]

The combination of intelligence and toughness earned Ron Mix the nickname "Intellectual Assassin." Despite playing in the obscurity of an offensive line, he had the ultimate résumé for a football player. He was named college All-American, selected nine times to the Pro Bowl, and inducted into the Pro Football Hall of Fame. Mix was a number one draft choice of both National football and American football franchises in the era before the two competing leagues merged. His choice of the upstart American Football League was viewed by many analysts as a factor that led to a merger. His signing convinced owners in the established National Football League that the bidding war would ultimately cost them more top players than they had anticipated.

Nine times Mix was selected as All-Pro. He played in five championship games and was voted into the Pro Football Hall of Fame.

Ron Mix was arguably the greatest of-fensive lineman in football history. (Photo courtesy of the San Diego Chargers, by Charles Aqua Viva.)

In a letter to me dated June 26, 1973, Mix wrote:

The general mass of people admire daring, courage, and tenacity. . . . Intellectual accomplishments have never been among the most honored qualities. Indeed, the general feeling is that physical prowess and intellectual accomplishments are mutually exclusive.

It has been part of the Jewish stereotype to equate Jews with intellectuals; ergo, not then equated with physical prowess. Well, Jews take the same pride in physical accomplishment as others and thus have been undoubtedly troubled by this phase of their stereotype, just as they have been troubled by other phases.

Thus the Jew is likely to take a racial pride in the accomplishments of a Jewish athlete. I have witnessed this during my career as a professional football player. Jewish youngsters and adults have approached me and were clearly pleased that I was a Jewish athlete.

To carry this observation further, but cast in a different light, witness the great pride that world Jewry takes in the accomplishments of Israel and the collective Israeli reputation for hard work, fighting, courage, and daring. The emergence of Israel has completely changed the stereotype of the Jew and allowed him to function comfortably in American society.

In the end, however, I would caution young people that there is no personal merit in the accomplishments of others. For a minority group, racial pride is inevitable. But realistically, the achievements of others do not make the non-achieving observer any better. One must look to themselves and take pride in their own work, their own attitudes, and actions.

There is no guarantee that tomorrow you will not be a victim of an injustice you allow to exist today. All people have a responsibility to call attention to injustices that exist anywhere within world society. That one is a potential victim, of course, makes the interest in doing so more personal; but, the fervor should be the same. We truly do live in a world community wherein isolated events affect all eventually. Thus, there is a selfish reason to correct injustices even if one is motivated altruistically.

Public figures have a podium not reserved for others and their efforts—even if not in degree any greater than others—have a wider span of influence. Yes, Jewish superstars should use this podium to the same extent as their peers of other faiths. . . . When one is young, most encounters of prejudice are imagined because one is sensitive to being different; and I experienced the same discomfort when one imagines himself to be in a foreign situation—in my case, a Jew within a predominately Christian country. The feeling lasts only until the one belonging to the minority group matures enough to realize that if some people harbor general prejudices against others then that is their problem.

NUMBER 6
SHAWN GREEN [50, PROJECTED]

Outfielder Shawn Green was quietly selected by baseball's Toronto Blue Jays as the sixteenth overall pick of the first round in the June 1991 free-agent draft. He quickly became a regular in

While with the Toronto Blue Jays, Shawn Green took pride in becoming the first Jewish baseball player to hit thirty home runs and steal thirty bases in the same season—a combination made famous by Bobby Bonds. In 2002, Green's home run power and speed began to earn comparisons of him with Bobby's son, Barry. (Photo courtesy of the Los Angeles Dodgers.)

the big leagues with the solid batting average and above-average power that had been expected of him.

Then, he blossomed unexpectedly as a superstar by hitting 42 homers and batting .309 in 1999 after becoming the first Jew to combine 30 homers and 30 stolen bases the previous year—an ethnic distinction he expressed pride in achieving. Green's earning power forced a trade to the Los Angeles Dodgers, who signed him to a contract of $84 million over six years. At the time, he was the second-highest-paid player ever in Major League Baseball.

In 2001, Green slugged 49 home runs and early in 2002 hit 22 home runs in a thirty-four-game span—including 4 in one game wrapped around a double and single—and another 4 in consecutive at bats over two games.

He has the potential to warrant a ranking within or just after the top five Jewish athletes of all time by making the National Baseball Hall of Fame. The ranking is based on a projected career of one year of 56 or more home runs, two years of 40 to 55 home runs with a .300 to .339 batting average, four years of 40 to 55 home runs with a .270 to .299 batting average, two years of 30 to 39 home runs with a .270 to .299 batting average, and selection to six All-Star teams.

Green has followed the precedent set by Hank Greenberg and Sandy Koufax by not playing on either Rosh Hashanah or Yom Kippur.

NUMBER 7
BENNY LEONARD [49]

The "Ghetto Wizard," Benny Leonard was arguably the greatest pound-for-pound boxer ever to set foot in a ring.

Leonard won the World Lightweight Boxing Championship on May 28, 1917, and achieved a rare accomplishment for a boxer by retiring as champion on January 15, 1925. His comeback nearly seven years later as a welterweight nearly landed him another championship belt. Leonard smiled at welterweight champion Jack Britton and knocked him down with a lightning combination— only to lose by disqualification for hitting Britton again before he could rise.

To get an eyewitness description of Leonard, I turned to Barney Kremenko, who for decades worked as a sports reporter and columnist for several major newspapers before becoming director of public relations for the New York Nets basketball team. This was his response:

> I think Benny Leonard made the strongest impact of any Jew in boxing. Leonard, coming from the East Side of New York . . . was suave, debonair, extremely clever, and a good puncher as well. He had patent leather hair always neatly combed; and the legend about him was that you were in your greatest trouble when you ruffled his hair. His boxing set a pattern and it is my belief that Sugar Ray Robinson later became the ultimate Benny Leonard.

In 1974, I received a letter from Sam Taub—the famous boxing announcer of his day. An institution in sports, he had called some of the most famous fights in history on radio broadcasts heard throughout the nation. The voice and patented style of Sam Taub were as immediately recognizable to fight fans in his era as Howard Cosell's would be years later.

Taub named more than two dozen athletes in sports ranging from baseball, football, and basketball to boxing before revealing to me his selection as the greatest Jewish athlete of all time. I had asked him to name the greatest Jewish boxer he had ever seen. Taub was resolute and unequivocal in his response: "There is only one who would fit that description; his name is Benny Leonard."

From his early days as a ring announcer, Taub recalled Benny Leonard as not only the greatest Jewish boxer he had ever seen but the greatest Jewish athlete as well.

In Nat Fleischer's 1962 Ring Record Book and Boxing Encyclopedia, *Benny Leonard is ranked as the second greatest lightweight of all time. A study of the penetrating intensity from Benny Leonard creates a chilling three-dimensional illusion that his left fist is reaching out of the photograph with a lightning jab. (Photo courtesy of* Ring Magazine.*)*

NUMBER 8
KEN HOLTZMAN
[46, PROJECTED]

As a rookie with the Chicago Cubs, Ken Holtzman handed the legendary Sandy Koufax his final regular season defeat. During the next few years, he pitched no-hitters against both an Atlanta Braves team featuring Hank Aaron and a Cincinnati Reds team with Johnny Bench. Not even that could satisfy Cub manager Leo Durocher, who had inexplicably traded Sid Gordon away from the New York Giants two decades earlier. Durocher had a personality conflict with Holtzman as well and traded the Jewish pitcher to the Oakland A's, for whom he immediately blossomed into a superstar.

In a letter to me dated April 28, 1973, Holtzman made this apparent reference to his days playing under Durocher:

> Nobody feels the sting of prejudice like some professional athletes. One day—when I'm out of the game—I'll tell it like it was. The night I learned about Munich [at the 1972 Olympics] was the night before I was to pitch in Chicago. I was with Mike Epstein and— needless to say—we were shocked. I think we felt angry at first and then grief. We knew some crackpot could be after one of us. We decided to wear black arm bands the next day at the game, although neither of us felt like playing. We wore the bands for about a week, realizing this could mark us. But, it didn't matter.

By the time he was thirty, Holtzman had already won 165 regular season games, two league championship games, and four World Series games—including three opening day games in a row. He had compiled stunning earned run averages of 2.06 in league championship games and 2.55 in World Series games. He pitched two no-hitters and even hit a World Series home run. Holtzman never experienced arm problems. It was reasonable to anticipate that he would increase his 165 games won to 300—the level that traditionally ensures entrance into the National Baseball Hall of Fame. Then Holtzman was traded to the reigning World Series champion New York Yankees.

With textbook perfect form, Ken Holtzman is about to deliver. During his three full seasons with the Oakland A's, Ken Holtzman averaged twenty regular season wins with an earned run average of below 3 runs per game. He won the opening game of the World Series each of those years in leading the team to three consecutive championships. (Photo courtesy of the Oakland A's.)

Although it might have seemed that the Holtzman's career would flourish in the New York spotlight, his pitching opportunities were significantly diminished. In *The Bronx Zoo* (Crown, 1979), a book coauthored with Peter Golenbock, former Yankee reliever Sparky Lyle predicted that Holtzman would never be able to pitch effectively again.

Lyle was right. After his stay with the Yankees and ill-fated tour under Billy Martin, it was back to Chicago—from where the demoralized Jewish southpaw opted for a premature retirement. The forced inactivity enabled Holtzman to win only nine more games in sporadic appearances over two years. The sting of ostracism showed in Holtzman's pained expression in both his Yankee and Cub team photographs. In the 1980 book, *Number 1*, by Martin and sportswriter Peter Golenbock (Delacorte), the late Yankee manager took issue with then Kansas City manager Whitey Herzog for implying the obvious—that Martin should have pitched Holtzman.

Holtzman was at the midpoint of a Hall of Fame career when he joined the Yankees and is ranked here on the projection of what he would have achieved if he had the opportunity to complete it instead of being forced into a constructive termination.

Inducting Ken Holtzman into the National Baseball Hall of Fame would follow the current practice of admitting discriminated African Americans whose statistics would not otherwise warrant it. An example is Monte Irvin, who began his major league career at thirty and played seven years with a .293 batting average and 99 home runs.

Holtzman was given what in legal terms is known as a "constructive termination" that was the result of disparate treatment than that afforded the team's other potential Hall of Fame players—Catfish Hunter, Reggie Jackson, Ron Guidry, Goose Gossage, Sparky Lyle, and Thurman Munson—all of whom, like Holtzman, were in their prime but, unlike Holtzman, were Gentile. Those Gentile players were always given the opportunity to

Ken Holtzman pitching in the fabled Yankee pinstripes. (Photo courtesy of the New York Yankees.)

play; Holtzman was not. Had Holtzman not been constructively terminated, he stood to have nine more years that were likely to have been commensurate with the nine years that had just passed.

The Record and Projected Record of Ken Holtzman

Year	Innings	SO	Wins	Losses	ERA Career Record
(1965–1979: Cubs, A's, Orioles, Yankees, and Cubs)					
	2,867	2,601	174	150	3.49
Best Five Years					
1970	288	202	17	11	3.38
1972	265	134	19	11	2.51
1973	297	157	21	13	2.97
1974	255	117	19	17	3.07
1975	266	122	18	14	3.14
Composite					
	274	146	19	13	3.02

Career When Adding in Nine Years Lost When Given a "Constructive Termination"

Actual Record before Discrimination:
(1965–1976)   165   135

Imputed Record for Holtzman's Years Missed:

Missed Year	Year Actual	Wins	Losses	Earned Run Average
1977	(1968)	11	14	3.35
1978	(1969)	17	13	3.59
1979	(1970)	17	11	3.38
1980	(1971)	9	15	4.48
1981	(1972)	19	11	2.51
1982	(1973)	21	13	2.97
1983	(1974)	19	17	3.07
1984	(1975)	18	14	3.14
1985	(1976)	14	11	3.65
		310	254	

Holtzman's No-hitters

Holtzman's First No-hitter

Chicago, August 19, 1969

Atlanta Braves	At bats	Hits
Alou cf	4	0
Millan 2b	4	0
H. Aaron rf	4	0
Carty lf	2	0
Cepeda 1b	3	0
Boyer 3b	3	0
Didier c	2	0
Garrido ss	2	0
Niekro p	2	0
T. Aaron ph	1	0
Niebauer p	0	0
Atlanta Braves	000 000 000—0	
Chicago Cubs	300 000 000—0	

Holtzman's Second No-hitter

Cincinnati, June 3, 1971

Cincinnati Reds	At bats	Hits
McRae lf	3	0
Helms 2b	4	0
L. May 1b	2	0
Bench c	3	0
T. Perez 3b	3	0
Foster cf	3	0
Bradford rf	1	0
Concepcion ss	3	0
Nolan p	2	0
Ferrara ph	0	0
Gibbon p	0	0
Chicago Cubs	001 000 000—1	
Cincinnati Reds	000 000 000—0	

The obvious way to make Ken Holtzman whole is for Major League Baseball to reevaluate his Hall of Fame credentials by adding in the actual records of his previous nine seasons for the years 1977 to 1985. That would put Holtzman's win total above the obligatory 300.

The Case for Inducting Ken Holtzman into the National Baseball Hall of Fame

I presented the case to two rabbis for inducting Ken Holtzman into the National Baseball Hall of Fame on the precedents that have already been set for admitting black athletes who suffered discrimination. The same judgment was quickly reached and unequivocally conveyed by Rabbi Stuart L. Berman of Temple Shalom in Flushing, New York, and Rabbi Levi Deitsch of Chabad at Tysons in McLean, Virginia. Both Rabbis Berman and Deitsch stated that Holtzman should be inducted.

Rabbi Deitsch had this to say about the case for inducting Ken Holtzman into the National Baseball Hall of Fame under the precedents established for admitting discriminated African Americans:

The very reason why I established a Jewish synagogue in the predominantly Gentile area of Virginia is because of the situation such as that in which Ken Holtzman found himself in being obviously discriminated against and isolated in a world of baseball that in-

Pitcher Ken Holtzman appears to find humor in what future Rabbi Stuart L. Berman of Temple Shalom in Flushing, New York, is saying. The subject was obviously not Leo Durocher or Billy Martin. Rabbi Berman agreed that precedents set to remedy discrimination for members of the old Negro Leagues should be applied to put Holtzman in the Baseball Hall of Fame. (Photo courtesy of Rabbi Stuart L. Berman.)

Rabbi Levi Deitsch, founder of a northern Virginia synagogue, Chabad at Tysons, is shown here with his wife Miriam and children Chaya and Mendel. (Photo courtesy of Rabbi Levi Deitsch.)

cludes a small proportion of Jewish players. Surely, the injustice that Holtzman suffered should be handled in the only equitable way possible and by precedents already set—that is, to put him in the Hall of Fame.

NUMBER 9
DICK SAVITT [41, PROJECTED]

At Cornell University, Dick Savitt posted a career singles record that landed him in the Collegiate Tennis Hall of Fame with fifty-seven wins and two losses. Then he burst into prominence on the professional circuit by emerging as the 1951 Wimbledon singles champion, Australian Open singles champion, and the Italian Open doubles co-winner.

No professional tennis player had ever won all three of those tournaments in a single year, and Savitt was only the second to

*Dick Savitt retired prematurely after winning Wimbledon,
so his ranking reflects an adjustment of his points as if he
had won it a second time. (Photo courtesy of Cornell University.)*

have won two. Yet, he was inexplicably not selected to play in the
Davis Cup Challenge Round that year—a year in which the
United States went down to defeat in a loss that very possibly
could have been averted if Savitt had not been bypassed.

The story sounds as if it were a prelude to baseball pitching
star Kenny Holtzman's league championship and World Series
inexplicable benching, while his New York Yankees went down
to defeat twenty-five years later. Just as Holtzman would, a bit-
ter Dick Savitt opted for a premature retirement in disgust at
twenty-five.

Five years after gaining admittance to the International Tennis
Hall of Fame, at fifty-four, Savitt and his son won the U.S. father

and son doubles title. Despite having won the most prestigious of all tennis tournaments at Wimbledon, Savitt was quoted as calling the victory with his son as his most important win.

Savitt is ranked here as if he had won Wimbledon twice on the premise that had he not been forced into premature retirement, he would have won it at least one more time again; his point total reflects that interpretation.

NUMBER 10
BENNY FRIEDMAN
[39, PROJECTED]

Benny Friedman belongs in the Pro Football Hall of Fame and is ranked as if he had made it.

A two-time All-American and four-time All-NFL quarterback, Friedman launched football's first great passing attack out of the old single-wing formation used before Sid Luckman's introduction of the T-formation.

Legendary Notre Dame coach Knute Rockne described Friedman as "the greatest passer of all time" and "a standout runner and blocker." He was also an accurate field goal kicker.

As the highest salaried player of his era, Friedman single-handedly turned around the New York Giants. From the worst team in the league, Friedman made them a powerhouse.

Friedman was denied the ultimate honor of his sport, entrance into the Pro Football Hall of Fame. The assessment of Friedman by Knute Rockne turned out to be ironic. Rockne's career was the subject of a movie featuring future president Ronald Reagan as dying football star George Gipp; and Gipp's final words, as portrayed by Reagan, now take on special meaning, particularly if a rightful place is ever made in the Pro Football Hall of Fame for Friedman. Perhaps, like Gipp, Friedman will know about it and be happy.

Two days before Thanksgiving in 1982—after making critical statements about his exclusion that were published in the *New York Times*—Friedman put a gun to his head and shot himself dead.

Benny Friedman was denied the ultimate honor of his sport, entrance into the Pro Football Hall of Fame. (Photo courtesy of Benny Friedman, by Fabian Bachrach.)

In a letter to me dated June 12, 1973, Friedman stated:

There definitely was a Jewish following. Jews naturally look to those who are outstanding in a sport and identify with them. I believe that religion should be left private. A youngster or adult plays a game as a competitor, with no reflection about his faith. It just happens that one is a Jew or Catholic, or what not. I never felt that I was a spokesman. I did represent to the Jewish people a breakthrough when I was elected captain of Michigan, in 1926. The Jews were concerned about whether I would be elected, but I was not.

I never was threatened and I never had any anti-Jewish experiences. My teammates and opponents were wonderful. In athletics, there is a common denominator of dedication to a team that transcends all else. One gives and takes and performs and is recognized by his performance, not by any outside circumstances.

My mother helped me in her way by her faith. She felt that 18—representing Chai, which means life—was needed in this charity gesture to protect me. I was never injured and I never questioned about this representation of her faith. It worked.

NUMBER 11
LOU BOUDREAU [37]

A slick fielding and consistent-hitting shortstop with occasional power, Lou Boudreau won a Most Valuable Player award as player-manager of the Cleveland Indians and was named to four All-Star teams.

Boudreau designed an innovative shift to defend against the legendary Ted Williams and finally joined him as a teammate with the Boston Red Sox for the last season of his career before joining Williams again in the National Baseball Hall of Fame.

Even though it had been common knowledge that Boudreau's mother was a Jew, in 1989, I followed the precedent of all earlier authors of major books on Jewish athletes by making no mention of his mother's Judaism while he was still alive. My 1989 book *The Jewish Athletes' Hall of Fame* made no mention of Boudreau's name at all.

In 2002, I asked Indians's media relations director Bart Swain why that precedent had been set. Swain cited Cleveland sports

Lou Boudreau completed his career with the Boston Red Sox after twelve Hall of Fame years in Cleveland, where he attracted a large Gentile following as a playing manager with the Indians. (Photo courtesy of the Boston Red Sox.)

historian Hal Lebovitz in advising me that "Boudreau's mother was indeed Jewish, but he did not practice the religion and never admitted to being of the Jewish faith."

I asked Swain whether Boudreau had expressed a desire not to be associated with Jewish people or whether he had merely wanted privacy.

"The part about him not wanting to be identified seems to be the case according to Mr. Lebovitz," Swain replied.

NUMBER 12
BUDDY MYER [34, PROJECTED]

Buddy Myer reigned as a league leader in hitting and record-setting second baseman in the field for the old Washington Nationals with a better than .300 lifetime batting average for parts of seventeen years.

In 1935, he led the American League with a .349 batting average and batted in 100 runs. He established a major league record in fielding with 138 double plays. Myer was named to two All-Star teams.

On the basis of pure statistics, the careers of Myer at second base and that of Lou Boudreau decades later, at shortstop, were very similar. The two neighboring positions of shortstop and second base carried similar expectations of good fielding and adequate hitting that both players substantially exceeded.

Both players carried outstanding gloves and consistently demonstrated better than merely adequate hitting. Their respective career batting and fielding averages had a less than 10-point variance, but Boudreau did not play as long as did Myer and consequently had almost 400 fewer base hits. In compiling a .303 lifetime batting average, as compared to Boudreau's .295 average, Myer hit .300 or better nine times; Boudreau reached the level four times.

Both Lou Boudreau and Buddy Myer had outstanding careers, but Myer was a demonstratively better player. In a travesty of justice, Myer never made the National Baseball Hall of Fame. Boudreau did. Myer is ranked here, in the All-Time Ranking of Great Jewish Athletes, as if he had. Boudreau's induction into the

National Baseball Hall of Fame provides a justification that Buddy Myer should now be inducted, too.

NUMBER 13
BARNEY ROSS [32]

Ross's given name was Barnet David Rasofsky; but he took the name Barney Ross after seeing his devout Jewish father shot to death in a mob-directed robbery of his Chicago grocery store and being talked into a boxing career by then welterweight champion Jackie Fields—another in the long line of Jewish champions, who had changed his name from Jacob Finklestein.

Ross, ranked as the ninth greatest welterweight of all time by Nat Fleischer, was a hero to many but a villain to himself. In 1933, he became the first boxer ever to hold two championships simultaneously.

Over the course of a thirteen-year career, he held three titles—the world lightweight, world junior welterweight, and world welterweight—and was never knocked out. Ross was inducted into the International Boxing Hall of Fame.

In modern boxing, there are not only more weight class divisions than when Barney Ross fought but usually several champions recognized by competing organizations in each class. It is rare now to see a unified champion, even in weight divisions of less range. During World War II, Ross joined the U.S. Marine Corps and was awarded the Silver Star. In 1957, a movie entitled *Monkey on My Back* depicted his life. Actor Cameron Mitchell portrayed Ross as a tragic narcotics addicted fighter.

NUMBER 14
NAT HOLMAN [30]

During the teens, Nat Holman burst into prominence as the first pure point guard in professional basketball history. Until then,

Nat Holman served as president of the U.S. Committee on Sports for Israel. (Photo courtesy of Nat Holman.)

teams operated without a specific player designated as primary ball handler, and no one individual was looked upon to distribute the ball.

He is credited with scoring the first recorded "triple double"— a subsequently categorized statistical term coined by 1980s basketball star Magic Johnson to reflect a combination of double-digit numbers in points, assists, and rebounds. Holman's leadership was the guiding force behind the first great Boston Celtic championship team.

In addition to the original Celtics, Holman played for professional teams in Brooklyn, Syracuse, and Chicago. For having been arguably the most savvy ball handler ever to grace a basketball court, Holman was inducted into the Naismith Memorial Basketball Hall of Fame.

In 1950, a Holman-coached City College of New York team of five similarly sized players adopted his innovative "interchangeable parts strategy" to become the only college team ever to win the NIT and NCI titles in a single season. Almost twenty-five years later, I wrote Holman and asked whether Jewish athletes have an obligation to be role models for Jewish youth. "I believe that Jewish athletes can be a powerful influence by setting examples and raising standards for youth and adults to achieve positive goals," he replied. "Qualities developed in athletic competition are the same qualities essential for success in all walks of life."

NUMBER 15
HARRIS BARTON
[28, PROJECTED]

The product of a devoutly religious Jewish family, Harris Barton attended a Jewish school and was bar mitzvahed and confirmed. He

Harris Barton was selected to two All-Pro teams and started on the San Francisco Giant offensive line that won the 1995 Super Bowl. (Photo courtesy of the San Francisco 49ers.)

was a number one draft choice after being named All-American at the University of North Carolina, and he finished second in Rookie of the Year balloting his first season, a rare feat for the comparative anonymity of his position. He also twice made All-Pro in the National Football League.

Barton was integral to the offensive line that enabled the also religious Mormon quarterback Steve Young to lead the San Francisco 49ers to a blowout Super Bowl victory. He is projected to make the Pro Football Hall of Fame and is ranked accordingly.

NUMBER 16
BATTLING LEVINSKY [27]

From 1916 through 1920, Battling Levinsky reigned as world light heavyweight boxing champion. With a real surname of Lebrowitz, he was the largest Jewish boxer ever to hold a title. At five feet eleven inches and some 175 pounds, Levinsky stood four inches taller and weighed fifteen pounds more than the only Jewish world heavyweight champion—Daniel Mendoza, who reportedly held the title from 1791 through 1795. In 1918, Levinsky stepped up to the heavyweight division for a shot at the legendary Jack Dempsey's title and stunned the sellout crowd by flooring Dempsey not once but twice in round 4 before being knocked out in the next round by the legendary heavyweight champion. It would be the closest Dempsey would ever come to being knocked out.

Two years later, Levinsky lost a close decision to Gene Tunney some seven years before Tunney's survival of a long-count that enabled him to end Dempsey's reign as undefeated heavyweight champion.

NUMBER 17
AL ROSEN [25]

In a letter from Al Rosen to me dated July 5, 1973, he wrote:

There is no doubt that a Jewish athlete, if he has any degree of success in his career, picks up a large Jewish following. It is a warm feeling to demonstrate those ideas that can be exemplary amongst Jews.

I have always attempted to be honest and forthright when questioned about the Jewish issues in the world. I have worked long and hard in the community at attempting to justify my existence and I feel that it is incumbent upon Jews everywhere to become well-known spokesmen for the Jewish religion. I feel that Jewish athletes, particularly because of the publicity given to their acts, should always be aware of their heritage and act accordingly.

In 1953, Hank Greenberg had been the only player in history ever to be unanimously selected American League Most Valuable Player. Rosen became the second by slugging 43 home runs, driving in 145 runs, and batting .336 as an excellent-fielding

Ethnic slurs may have been the reason for a premature retirement by Al Rosen at thirty-two, while still at his prime. It likely cost him entrance into the National Baseball Hall of Fame. (Photo courtesy of Al Rosen.)

third baseman. The following year, he hit 2 home runs in the All-Star game—a game that happened to be held in Cleveland. During a five-year span, Rosen averaged better than 31 homers with 114 runs batted in while hitting at a better than .298 clip. In taking over third base for the Indians, Rosen replaced a popular Ken Keltner—the one made famous by two spectacular diving stops of would-be base hits that ended Joe DiMaggio's incredible fifty-six-game hitting streak in 1941.

As an extraordinary consequence of his also being Jewish in an era of anti-Semitism, Rosen never escaped booing by his home team fans and ethnic slurs by those who were anti-Semites. The ethnic slurs may have been the reason for a premature retirement at thirty-two, while still at his prime, which likely cost him entrance into the National Baseball Hall of Fame.

After his career, Rosen held executive positions with several major league clubs. He served as team president of the New York Yankees over a fellow Jew in Gabe Paul over manager Billy Martin. Eventually, Rosen resigned. Paul had already left.

Rosen later rebuilt a San Francisco Giants team with a losing record and took it to the World Series—a feat that would result in Rosen being named Executive of the Year.

NUMBER 18
MARSHALL GOLDBERG [22]

Marshall Goldberg achieved All-America distinctions, in 1937 as a halfback and again in 1938 at fullback. At either position and as a kickoff returner, Goldberg was a breakaway threat with the potential to go all the way. As a professional, he played for a Chicago Cardinal team that used him primarily as a defense back. In 1941, Goldberg led the National Football League with 7 interceptions in an eight-game season and kickoff return yardage as well. He played on the Cardinal team that won the NFL championship in 1948 and was named All-Pro three times.

Mr. and Mrs. Marshall Goldberg celebrate a night on the town. (Photo courtesy of Marshall Goldberg.)

NUMBER 19
TED "KID" LEWIS [22]

Ted "Kid" Lewis won the World Welterweight Boxing Championship in Boston in 1915 and again in Dayton, Ohio, in 1917. He held the title for the next two years. Although just under five feet six inches and weighing about 125 pounds, Lewis fought exhibitions against light heavyweight and heavyweight contenders. His battles against Jack Britton created a rivalry that defined a place for Ted "Kid" Lewis in boxing history—much like battles with Joe Frazier would someday define the greatness of Muhammad Ali.

Although Lewis was British, he fought mostly in the United States and is included in these rankings for that reason. Lewis held the world welterweight crown for three years in the last half of the decade of the teens. He was rated by Nat Fleischer as the fourth greatest welterweight of all time.

NUMBER 20
AMY ALCOTT [21]

The year was 1992 and it involved something that a popular Jewish athlete had reportedly said. The commentary came from Rush Limbaugh. A woman golfer had dropped out of a major tournament upon hearing of the death of her companion poodle. Limbaugh ridiculed not only that woman but a more famous woman golfer as well for her touching expression of condolence and support. Then he mimicked both of them in an exaggerated infantile voice.

The more famous woman golfer was Amy Alcott—an articulate defender of both animals and people who are oppressed. When former CBC golf commentator Ben Wright had made disparaging remarks about women golfers, Alcott was quoted by the Associated Press as replying, "His comments brought out a lot of the old stereotypes connected to women athletes. There's so

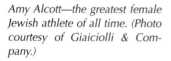
Amy Alcott—the greatest female Jewish athlete of all time. (Photo courtesy of Giaiciolli & Company.)

much more to us than that." She did not even dignify the remarks of Limbaugh. Throughout her career, Amy Alcott has always exuded a maturity that elevated her above that type of exchange.

A reason may be because of the unusually young age that she attained stardom. As a twenty-one-year-old in only her third professional golf tournament, Alcott had stunned the sports world with an upset victory at the 1975 Orange Blossom Classic. Four years later, she won the Canadian Open. When she captured the U.S. Open the following year, in 1980, Alcott had become a superstar. She then solidified that status with victories at the Nabisco Dinah Shore Tournament in 1983, 1988, and 1991.

Alcott gained entrance into the Ladies Professional Golfers Hall of Fame with 35 points based on rigid criteria of winning a sanctioned event, maintaining the lowest scoring average over an entire year, and winning a major. To gain entrance, a golfer must accumulate 27 points, and few ever reach that. Amy Alcott is the greatest female Jewish athlete of all time.

NUMBER 21
COREY PAVIN [21]

Corey Pavin scored victories early in his career at the Houston Coca-Cola Open, the Greater Milwaukee Open, and the Colonial National Invitation at a staggering fourteen under par. By 1985, he soared to sixth place on the money list and stayed around that level for two years. Suddenly, Pavin lost his magic touch and slumped out of the rankings. When his game suddenly returned, it returned to an astronomical level. In 1991, Pavin was named the Professional Golfer's Association's Player of the Year and emerged as the tour's top money winner. He became the first Jewish golfer to win a major by winning the U.S. Open in 1995, four years after reportedly converting to a Gentile religion. On August 8, 1995, the *New York Times* quoted Pavin's observation that his victory in the U.S. Open had demonstrated that he had not become less competitive as a result of his conversion some four years earlier.

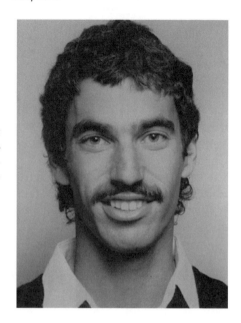

Until Corey Pavin won the 1995 U.S. Open, he was known as the greatest golfer never to win a major. (Photo courtesy of the International Management Group.)

NUMBER 22

MAXIE ROSENBLOOM [20]

Maxie Rosenbloom may have been the inspiration for Muhammad Ali's "rope-a-dope." Rosenbloom slapped his way to the World Light Heavyweight Championship and held onto the title for four years until a fellow Jew, Bob Olen, outpointed him by standing back and forcing Rosenbloom out of his shell. More than four decades later, first Ali and then Jimmy Young adopted Rosenbloom's open-glove style of blocking punches against a young George Foreman. Ali leaned against the ropes in what he called a "rope-a-dope" and let the then champion Foreman punch himself into exhaustion before knocking him out. Young ruined Foreman's first comeback attempt by humiliating him into a hiatus for a decade with a sloppy majority decision. History almost repeated itself when the Olen tactic nearly enabled journeyman Ron Lyle to upset Ali, until he rallied late for a technical knockout of Lyle.

NUMBER 23
LYLE ALZADO [20]

In his book, *Mile High* (Atheneum, 1978), Lyle Alzado wrote about his Jewish mother but was televised wearing a cross fourteen years later when news of his impending death became public. Playing both defensive end and tackle, the six foot three inch, 254-pound Alzado began his career with the Denver Broncos in 1971. He stayed with the Broncos until being traded to the Cleveland Browns in 1979. Alzado joined the Oakland Raiders in 1982 and led the team to a Super Bowl victory.

Alzado retired as one of the greatest defensive linemen ever to play the game. Yet he may have chosen the wrong sport. As an amateur heavyweight boxer, he won twenty-seven straight bouts and later performed credibly in a boxing exhibition against then-champion Muhammad Ali.

In materials provided by publicists before his fatal cancer was diagnosed, Lyle Alzado was quoted as saying, "I believe that the greatest sacrifice brings the greatest success." Little did he know that the sacrifice he had paid in taking steroids to become a great football player would soon come back and take his life. (Photo courtesy of Winokur, Ryder Public Relations.)

The real-life story of Lyle Alzado imitated art, borrowing a page from the book *The Year the Yankees Lost the Pennant*, which later became the classic movie *Damn Yankees*. Alzado sold his future for steroids that enabled him to overpower offensive lines and terrorize quarterbacks in the National Football League. Before he died, Alzado went public with his steroid use to dissuade other athletes from making the same fatal mistake.

NUMBER 24
ABE ATTELL [19, ADJUSTED]

Abe Attell won the World Featherweight Championship with a knockout in 1901 and held onto it until 1912—when he lost his title in a twenty-round decision. He was rated by Nat Fleischer as the third-greatest featherweight of all time. To keep his extraordinary accomplishments in proper context, only a third of the points compiled by Attell were applied in ranking him. Attell won less than half of the nearly eighty fights in which he engaged during his nearly eleven-year reign. There were not as many great fighters in the featherweight division as, for example, were in Benny Leonard's lightweight class.

NUMBER 25
MAX ZASLOFSKY
[18, PROJECTED]

In 1974, I asked Max Zaslofsky to cite his greatest accomplishment as a professional athlete. This was his response: "A few years ago, on the National Basketball Association's twenty-fifth anniversary, I was selected along with twenty-four other players as the twenty-five best players in the NBA for the last twenty-five years."

Max Zaslofsky—on the National Basketball Association's twenty-fifth anniversary, selected as one of the twenty-five best players in the NBA for the previous twenty-five years but excluded from the National Basketball Hall of Fame. (Photo courtesy of Max Zaslofsky.)

Zaslofsky led the National Basketball Association in scoring average in 1948 and free throws in 1950. He was selected to four All-Star squads.

In *Hank Greenberg: The Story of My Life* (Time Books, 1989), editor Ira Berkow quoted Sandy Koufax, who was also a great basketball player, as saying that his boyhood hero was Max Zaslofsky. At the Jewish Heritage Book Festival in New York, Berkow surprised many in the audience in revealing that fact. Many indicated that they had never heard of Zaslofsky and had just assumed that Koufax would have grown up idolizing Greenberg.

Although he retired in 1956 as the third-highest scorer in NBA history, Max Zaslofsky never was admitted to the National Basketball Hall of Fame. He is ranked here, in the All-Time Ranking of Great Jewish Athletes, as if he had.

NUMBER 26
HARRY NEWMAN [17]

Following closely behind Benny Friedman was Harry Newman—first as an All-America quarterback at the University of Michigan and then as an All-NFL quarterback with the New York Giants. As a rookie, Newman guided the Giants to a National Football League title in 1933 with thirteen consecutive completions and 2 touchdown passes. However, after running for more than a 100 yards in a game the following year, Newman's career abruptly ended with an injury.

I asked Max Winter, then chief executive of the Minnesota Vikings, to compare Newman with Benny Friedman and Sid Luckman. "I was fortunate to see them on several occasions. All three of them were very great quarterbacks and perhaps given the same chance to play on the same teams, I doubt there could be a great difference," he replied. Had Newman's career not abruptly ended, he might have gained proper credit for introducing the scrambling style that many modern quarterbacks adopted.

NUMBER 27
NANCY LIEBERMAN [17]

Nancy Lieberman was the youngest member of a 1976 United States Olympic women's basketball team, which won a silver medal. The five foot eleven inch-guard created mismatches in backcourt over much shorter women. Averaging around 4 steals a game, Lieberman was a three-time All-American and two-time Player of the Year. She led Old Dominion University to two intercollegiate championships with averages of more than 18 points and 9 rebounds a game. In the 1976 through 1977 academic year, she nearly averaged a triple double with a scoring average of 20.9 points, more than 10 rebounds, and almost 8 assists per game. Lieberman single-handedly elevated women's basketball and brought the sport an unprecedented national interest.

Nancy Lieberman was the first great women's basketball player. (Photo courtesy of Old Dominion University.)

In her book *Basketball My Way* (Scribner's, 1982), with Myrna and Harvey Frommer, Lieberman referred to her Jewish heritage; but in its review of my *Jewish Athletes' Hall of Fame* seven years later, the *National Jewish Post and Opinion* reported that Lieberman had "flirted" with a Gentile organization known as "Jews for Jesus." Lieberman was described as a devout Christian a decade later, in a book quoting her views on hypocrisy. She took pride in holding her own in scrimmages with members of the all-male National Basketball Association and helped launch professional women's basketball by playing in her late thirties for the Phoenix Mercury and then coaching the Detroit Shock.

After a losing 2000 season as coach of the Shock, Lieberman's contract was not renewed amid publication of unsubstantiated,

Slick ball-handling skills and tough post play landed Nancy Lieberman in the Basketball Hall of Fame. (Photo courtesy of Old Dominion University.)

vague, and irrelevant complaints by ineffectual players. On a basketball court, she could elude a trap in a drive down the lane; but because of her inescapably gentle and trusting nature, she never could avoid the hypocrites.

NUMBER 28
LOUIS "KID" KAPLAN [17]

In 1925, Louis "Kid" Kaplan won the World Featherweight Championship. He brought pride to his enormous Jewish following when it was revealed that he had rejected $50,000 to throw a fight.

Kaplan forfeited his title after eating his way out of that weight class. After moving up to the lightweight division, Kaplan beat the top contenders but was not given a title shot.

Kaplan was ranked by Nat Fleischer as the tenth-greatest featherweight of all time. The name "Kid" became so famous that many of the boxer's most ardent fans did not know Kaplan by his given first name of Louis.

NUMBER 29
JACKIE FIELDS [17]

After becoming the youngest athlete to win an Olympic gold medal with a series of victories at the 1924 Paris Olympics as a featherweight, Jackie Fields won the World Welterweight Boxing Championship in 1929. He won it again in 1932.

Fields was not ranked by Nat Fleischer as an all-time great, perhaps because his most memorable title defeat ended with him coiled on the canvas from an intentional foul by Joe Dundee.

The legendary Barney Ross credited Fields with guiding him into boxing after Ross's father had been slain while being robbed.

NUMBER 30
RUDY LARUSSO [16]

At six foot eight inches, Rudy LaRusso caused difficult match-ups for his opponents at small forward, who in his day were several inches shorter. He quickly fulfilled a potential for stardom at that position as the second selection in the 1959 National Basketball Association draft.

With the Los Angeles Lakers, LaRusso teamed with legends Elgin Baylor and Jerry West to create what many considered to the most explosive offensive trio ever to grace a basketball court. Unlike many modern small forwards with pure shooting skills, LaRusso moved constantly without the ball and played tenacious defense.

Some three decades later, guard Reggie Miller would draw frequent comparisons with LaRusso's shooting style because of the high arc and long distance to their shots, but LaRusso played before an extra point would be awarded for long-distance shooting. Had he played in the current era, LaRusso might have been a perennial contender for the scoring crown. LaRusso played in All-Star games in 1963, 1966, and 1968—a

Rudy LaRusso lets fly with one of his patented arching jump shots that made him unstoppable at Dartmouth. (Photo courtesy of Dartmouth College.)

year in which he averaged more than 20 points per game in both the regular season and playoffs for the San Francisco Warriors.

Although his mother was Jewish, LaRusso did not attract a large following among Jews during his career. Most people did not realize that he was Jewish. In a letter to me dated May 29, 1973, Los Angeles Lakers's publicity director Jeff Temkin wrote that to the best of his knowledge, "Rudy LaRusso is not Jewish, but Italian"; and former Dartmouth College sports information director Jack DeGange indicated he did not know.

NUMBER 31
ED NEWMAN [15]

The groans uttered by defensive tackles and blitzing linebackers was a precursor to the often-imitated greeting on a soon-to-come situation comedy for an unwelcome fat mailman by the same name.

But Ed Newman was a two-time All-Pro selection in the National Football League. And he was not fat.

Newman overcame two thyroid cancer operations to start at offensive guard for three Miami Dolphin Super Bowl teams—one of which was a championship winning team.

In addition to being named All-America in football at Duke University, Newman was a two-time Atlantic Coast Conference heavyweight wrestling champion.

Newman was also a power weight lifter with a bench press of 510 pounds. That strength enabled Newman to provide the Dolphins with the rugged power that helped hold opponents to only fourteen quarterback sacks in 1984.

In 1991, I appeared at the Miami Jewish Community Center when a gentleman remarked how he frequently saw "'Big Ed' jogging in the streets in as good a shape as ever." By then Newman had completed law school and already experienced success in his second professional career.

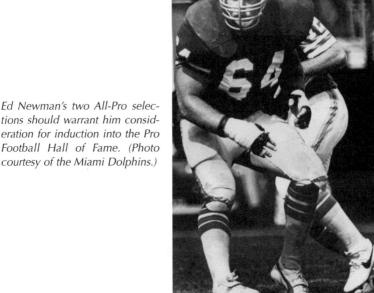

Ed Newman's two All-Pro selections should warrant him consideration for induction into the Pro
Football Hall of Fame. (Photo
courtesy of the Miami Dolphins.)

NUMBER 32
MARK SPITZ [14]

In the 1968 Olympics at Mexico City, Mark Spitz had already
won gold medals in two four-swimmer relays, a silver medal in
the 100-meter butterfly, and a bronze medal in the 100-meter
freestyle event when two African American medalists raised
their fists in protest of discrimination then of members of their
race in the United States. By the start of the 1972 Olympics in
Munich, speculation had evolved out of that demonstration
into an expectation that Spitz would make a profound statement to honor the six million Jews slaughtered by the host
country's former Nazi regime hardly more than three decades
earlier.

In 1972, Mark Spitz emerged as the greatest swimmer ever. Fifteen years later, I received a call from Herman Weiner, Spitz's father-in-law. He informed me that Spitz had maintained a presence in Jewish causes and was active in the Maccabiah Games. (Photo courtesy of the William Morris Agency.)

Spitz's only statement came in the form of gold medals. He won gold medals for his roles in three four-swimmer relays and four times individually in the 100-meter freestyle, the 100-meter butterfly, the 200-meter freestyle, and the 200-meter butterfly events. Seven gold medals had never been won in a single Olympiad in swimming, gymnastics, or track and field—the sports with opportunities to win that many.

Then, murdered in Munich were Jewish wrestlers Mark Slavin, eighteen, and Elizer Halfin, twenty-four; Jewish fencing coach Andre Spitzer, twenty-seven; Jewish weight lifters David Berger, twenty-eight, Ze'ev Friedman, thirty-two, and Joseph Roman, thirty-two; Jewish wrestling coach Moshe Weinberg, thirty-two; Jewish track and field coach Amitzur Shapita, forty; Jewish wrestling referee Yosef Gottfreund, forty; Jewish weight lifting referee Ya'acov Springer, fifty-two; and Jewish shooting coach Kehat Shorr, fifty-three. More than a quarter-century would pass, but various media treated as fresh news the publication of recollections about Spitz in 1972 by Bud Greenspan that "Mark lost points with the press with a series of 'no comments,' [and] the press gave him bad marks for being uncon-cerned" in the September 17, 1989, issue of *Parade*.

Greenspan's recollections corresponded with the record con-temporaneously published in the *1973 World Book Year Book*, which reported that "Spitz seemed curt and uninterested at news conferences, and he refused to pose with his seven gold medals (he sold the rights to a German magazine)."

Six months after the murders in Munich, Susan Lydon alleged in the March 11, 1973, edition of *New York Times Magazine* that Spitz had uttered a terribly insensitive remark that she quoted verbatim. Spitz was young and had been in mortal danger, pos-sibly in shock; and subsequent television interviews showed him to be clearly pained by both the Holocaust and the murders of Jews at the Olympics.

Almost two decades later, Spitz attempted a comeback. The April 1, 1991, edition of *USA Today* quoted him as saying, "Many

Edward Rosenblum, shown arriv-ing in the Soviet Union in 1958, attended six Olympics as an offi-cial of the United States Olympic Committee. (Photo courtesy of Edward Rosenblum.)

sports fans have pondered how would Joe Louis or Rocky Marciano have done against Muhammad Ali, or how would Babe Ruth have fared against today's pitchers?"

In August 1974, I interviewed Edward Rosenblum. He had been with Spitz at the 1968 Mexico City and 1972 Munich Olympics as an official of the United States Olympic Committee. These were his recollections:

> In Munich, Mark Spitz had matured. His adult attitude enabled him to win those seven gold medals. Mark Spitz, at that time, was an individualist; he was more for himself than anyone else, I am sorry to say. He was a loner. That's why Mark had such a disappointing showing. In Munich, Mark was a changed individual. He could adjust to his surroundings. He joined in with his fellow athletes and, as a result, was very highly thought of by others. I had the pleasure of meeting Mark's mother and father when they were with Mark. I'm happy to say that they are a typical Jewish family.

NUMBER 33
ISAAC BERGER [13]

In 1956, Isaac "Ice" Berger was the Olympic gold medalist in the weight lifting featherweight division. Berger went on to win silver medals in 1960 and 1964, when he jerked 336 pounds over his head. He military-pressed more than twice his 130-pound body weight. Berger was the strongest Jewish athlete of all time and may also have been the most religious.

Berger's father was a rabbi, and Berger became a cantor after his weight lifting days. There is no indication that Cantor Berger's congregation was anything but spiritually lifted by his singing or that his voice was ever off-key. Nevertheless, that evokes memories of heavyweight boxing champions Joe Frazier and Larry Holmes. No one ever had the nerve to tell them that they could not sing!

NUMBER 34
KENNY BERNSTEIN [12]

After unparalleled success during the eighties in Funny Car racing with thirty national event victories, Kenny Bernstein entered the nineties having switched to the more powerful but less dangerous Top Fuel class. He had won four consecutive National Hot Rod Association (NHRA) Funny Car Championships. Bernstein broke the 300-mile-per-hour barrier in 1992. He became the first race team owner to win championships in NHRA Winston Drag Racing, the NASCAR Winston Cup and IndyCar; and the first to win NHRA championships in both Top Fuel and Funny Car. Bernstein won his second NHRA Top Fuel championship in 2001. The following year, with retirement on the horizon, Bernstein won the Top Fuel title at the Sears Craftsman NHRA Nationals at his sponsor's Gateway International Raceway in Madison, Illinois.

Kenny Bernstein established himself as the greatest drag racer of all time. (Photo courtesy of Kenny Bernstein.)

NUMBER 35
RANDY GROSSMAN [11]

Tight end Randy Grossman played on four winning Super Bowl teams and contributed to each championship win. Playing for the Pittsburgh Steelers, Grossman emerged as quarterback Terry Bradshaw's favorite receiver for crucial short-yardage situations when a first down was needed to keep a drive alive. Grossman scored the first Steeler touchdown in Super Bowl X in 1975 against the Dallas Cowboys—a game that many analysts consider the most exciting Super Bowl ever. That Super Bowl touchdown followed a victorious American Conference Championship Game in which Grossman had caught 4 crucial passes. In 1978, he caught 37 passes and the following year averaged 18.1 yards per catch.

Randy Grossman was a clutch performer on one of the greatest football dynasties of all time. (Photo courtesy of the Pittsburgh Steelers.)

NUMBER 36
MATHIEU SCHNEIDER
[11, PROJECTED]

After having played on four National Hockey League teams, Mathieu Schneider instantly became a Hollywood idol when he joined the Los Angeles Kings because of his Jewish good looks. Skating at five feet ten inches and weighing less than two hundred pounds, Schneider often overpowers much larger opponents. If Howard Cosell were alive and called professional hockey, in his halting and often breathless voice, he might describe Schneider's non-stop action like this: "There is the pertinacious puck coverage that has made this man, Mathieu Schneider, so integral to his teams."

Over the course of thirteen years and still counting at thirty-one years old, Schneider has earned a reputation as one of the toughest defensemen in the National Hockey League. He was named to the Eastern Conference All-Star team for his rough play for the Islanders in 1996.

NUMBER 37
HARRY DANNING [10]

With good defense behind the plate and consistent hitting, Harry Danning built a solid reputation as a four-time National League All-Star in consecutive years for the New York Giants with a .285 lifetime batting average. For three consecutive years, Danning hit at a better than .300 pace.

Danning is best remembered for beating the Yankees in a 1937 World Series game with 3 base hits at the old Polo Grounds. His best regular-season games included one game in which he had 5 base hits and another in which he hit for the cycle—a single, double, triple, and home run. Many books have described an even greater early catcher, Johnny Kling, as Jewish; but a June 13, 1975, letter from Ken Smith, director of the National Baseball Hall of

Fame, advised that research by his librarian Jack Redding had revealed that only Kling's wife had been Jewish.

NUMBER 38
SID GORDON [10]

Unlike most power hitters, outfielder Sid Gordon was not streaky and did not strike out often. Gordon was a consistent .270 to .280 hitter, with 20 to 30 home runs and 80 to 100 runs batted in each year. He never struck out as many as fifty times in a season, which was highly unusual for someone who hit so many home runs.

Gordon's speed was below average, but he was an above-average fielder both in the outfield and at third base. Given his

For a home run hitter, Sid Gordon seldom struck out. (Photo courtesy of the Pittsburgh Pirates.)

ability to make contact at bat, a faster Gordon might have been able to win batting titles.

In his book *Five Seasons* (Simon & Schuster, 1977), Roger Angell recalls a newspaper story reporting why Gordon was traded in his prime in 1949, after putting together four solid seasons for the New York Giants. Gordon had attracted an enormous Jewish following—from both his Giant fans and cross-town rival Brooklyn Dodgers and was reaching his prime. According to Angell, Giants's chief executive Horace Stoneham was quoted in the story as saying that "Leo Durocher wanted his own kind of team."

That was the same Leo Durocher, of course, who would trade a Ken Holtzman in his prime more than two decades later. Both trades proved to be terrible mistakes. In his first year with the Boston Braves, Gordon responded by hitting .304 with 27 home runs and 103 runs batted in. He was walked seventy-eight times and struck out only thirty-one times, but was not selected for the All-Star team.

Gordon hit 2 home runs in one inning and 4 grand slams in the same year. He was the only player ever to pinch hit for the legendary Mel Ott.

NUMBER 39
HENRY WITTENBERG [10]

Four years after winning a gold medal in the 1948 Olympics as a free-style light heavyweight wrestler, Henry Wittenberg won a silver medal in an upset over the reigning Russian world champion August Englas. Wittenberg gained more prominence from the victory that earned him a silver medal than he had in winning the gold. Over a span of thirteen years, he won 400 consecutive matches.

Wrestling offers fewer medal-winning opportunities than swimming. Had Wittenberg gone on to win a second gold medal at the 1952 Olympics instead of the silver, he would have ranked as high as legendary swimmer Mark Spitz.

Henry Wittenberg brought his Olympic medals to Yeshiva University, where he served as wrestling coach. (Photo courtesy of Yeshiva University, by Herbert Sonnenfeld.)

NUMBER 40
MARK ROTH [9]

From the highest authority in his sport—the Professional Bowler's Association—comes acclaim that Mark Roth "is widely acknowledged as the father of the modern game" and observation that "his hard-throwing, hard-cranking style promulgated a generation of imitators that has made significant change in the nature of bowling." Roth entered the nineties as the major attraction of his sport, with the highest-scoring long-term pace ever set on the Professional Bowler's Association tour, with a better than 215-point-per-game average—an average dating back nearly fifteen years over more than eight thousand games.

It may be the similarity of their names and the fact that Mark Roth is also consid-ered the "father" of his sport, but there is a distinctive facial resemblance between him and Babe Ruth. (Photos courtesy of the Professional Bowler's Association and the New York Yankees.)

NUMBER 41
ERSKINE MAYER [8]

Erskine Mayer was a slowball pitcher who outsmarted hitters in a deadball era. He was signed by the Philadelphia Phillies in 1912 and quickly blossomed into a regular starting pitcher with a variety of slow pitches.

With pinpoint control, his spinning curveball came at different speeds to keep batters off balance. He won twenty-one games in 1914 and again in 1915 and ultimately retired with an earned run average of less than 3 runs per nine innings. His career started just two years before the signing of Babe Ruth as a pitcher by the Boston Red Sox and ended the year after Ruth was sold to the New York Yankees—where he entirely transformed the sport by slugging home runs at an unprecedented frequency.

Mayer was traded by the Phillies in 1918 to the Pittsburgh Pirates and picked up on waivers the following season by the infamous Chicago White Sox. Mayer was overshadowed with the Phillies by his legendary roommate, Grover Cleveland Alexander, a phenomenal pitcher, who would later be portrayed in a movie by future president Ronald Reagan. The low profile served Mayer well. He was never targeted with allegations concerning the conspiracy by some of his teammates to fix the 1919 World Series. Given the wide reign of anti-Semitism during that era, he was fortunate.

The best hitter of the Erskine Mayer era was not Jewish. Benny Kauff has been erroneously thought to be Jewish since he hit an astronomical .370 in 1914. He was permanently banned from the game by Major League Baseball commissioner K. M. Landis for unsubstantiated allegations of association with undesirable persons. An unprecedented lack of evidence in his ban may have been because of a misconception, as evidenced by enduring but entirely incorrect reporting over many years, that he was Jewish.

Neal Walk was widely reported to be a vegetarian in the 1970s, but his well-groomed bearded look in this photo gives him the appearance of someone from the Erskine Mayer Era. (Photo courtesy of the Phoenix Suns.)

NUMBER 42
NEAL WALK [7]

After being drafted second to Lew Alcinder—who achieved stardom as Kareem Abdul Jabbar—Neal Walk played five seasons for the Phoenix Suns. During the 1972–1973 season, Walk averaged 20.2 points per game and 12.4 rebounds. He played two seasons for the New York Knickerbockers and one in Israel. An operation to remove a benign spinal tumor left Walk paralyzed not long after he retired, but he resumed his basketball-playing career with the Samaritan Wheelchair Suns after that.

NUMBER 43
LEW TENDLER [7]

Lew Tendler gained recognition in many circles as the greatest fighter never to hold a crown and by Nat Fleischer as the ninth-greatest lightweight boxer of all time.

A year after fighting champion Benny Leonard to a brutal no decision ruling in 1922, Tendler came agonizingly close to capturing Leonard's world lightweight championship. Tendler staggered Leonard and had him on the verge of being knocked out, only to have Leonard somehow distract him into momentarily letting up.

Leonard pulled out a fifteen-round majority decision. The failed opportunity would haunt Lew Tendler for the rest of his days. Had Tendler won that fight, it would have been an extraordinary upset.

Instead of winning the World Lightweight Championship, Tendler merely joined a long list of defeated boxers whom Leonard had outsmarted.

NUMBER 44
STEVE STONE [7]

As a hot major league pitching prospect at Kent State University, Steve Stone played with catcher Thurman Munson—who would

Before fulfilling his potential with a twenty-five-win, Cy Young Award season with the Baltimore Orioles in 1980, Steve Stone bounced from team to team as a journeyman pitcher. (Photo courtesy of the San Francisco Giants.)

go on to become a colorful Yankee, only to die in a fiery plane crash at the peak of his career. I followed Stone to Kent State several years later and had the opportunity to read some poetry he had written. One poem told of an athlete who experienced fleeting success, but the glory was only borrowed. Little did he know that the poem would be a self-fulfilling prophesy; that he was describing the future of his own career.

After showing flashes of his potential greatness with a fifteen-win season three years earlier, Stone had a career year in 1980 with the Baltimore Orioles. He won the American League Cy Young Award with a spectacular twenty-five-win season, which included fourteen consecutive victories and a perfect three innings as a starting pitcher in the All-Star Game. Then, as in his poetry, Stone's arm went dead.

Stone stayed in the sport as a television announcer. During a Chicago Cubs game, he did the colorful commentary when President Ronald Reagan fulfilled a fantasy of his by calling a game.

On May 5, 1973, I received a letter from Stone, who had this to say: "Any Jewish athlete scared away from professional sports either lacks the drive or the intestinal fortitude to make it anyway." He also noted that "religion doesn't affect performance."

NUMBER 45
ART HEYMAN [7]

Art Heyman's honors as a college basketball player ranged from being named the 1963 NCI Player of the Year, selected three times as an All-American, and named Most Valuable Player of the NCI finals.

His greatest game came in his 1963 regular season finale. Heyman scored 40 points and hauled down 24 rebounds against North Carolina University.

At six feet five inches, Art Heyman lacked the size to exploit his power scoring style in the professional ranks. (Photo courtesy of Duke University.)

Being Jewish, Heyman seemed to be an ideal drawing attraction for the New York Knickerbockers. However, he never came close to the 25-point-per-game scoring average he had maintained over three years at Duke.

Heyman's six-season pro career included service with teams in both the National Basketball and upstart American Basketball Associations. His scoring averages ranged from the mid- to high teens.

NUMBER 46
JAY FIEDLER [7, PROJECTED]

Undrafted out of Dartmouth University in 1994 by any National Football League team, quarterback Jay Fiedler signed with the Philadelphia Eagles only to be cut after two years without a chance to play. Fiedler next signed with the Cincinnati Bengals and was promptly waived. Then came a stint with the Amsterdam Admirals of the World League.

With the Jacksonville Jaguars, Jay Fiedler readied himself to emerge in his next stop with the Miami Dolphins as a starting quarterback. (Photo courtesy of the Jacksonville Jaguars.)

Fiedler moved to the Minnesota Vikings and played only long enough to throw 7 passes at the end of five one-sided games because of the depth that team already had at the position. After moving to the Jacksonville Jaguars as a restricted free agent, starter Mark Brunell was injured, and Fiedler finally had a chance to play.

He completed nearly two-thirds of both his regular season and playoff passes in the reserve role. When future Hall of Famer Dan Marino retired, Fiedler signed with the Miami Dolphins to succeed him and finally opened a season as starting quarterback after five years in the league.

By going five games without an interception that year, Fiedler broke a team record that had been jointly held by Marino and an earlier Pro Football Hall of Fame quarterback, Bob Griese—who directed a Dolphin team that won consecutive Super Bowls, in January of 1973 and 1974. Griese, whose style of play Fiedler's most resembles, threw fewer touchdown passes than did Marino, but he also threw fewer interceptions and won much more often.

In the final game of 2000, Fiedler brought the Dolphins to a fourth-quarter come-from-behind victory. He completed 11 of 14 passes in the team's final two drives for the American Football Conference Eastern Division title.

In the opening round of the playoffs the next week, Fiedler completed 10 of 16 passes in the fourth quarter and overtime to give the Dolphins another win and himself a place on the cover of *Sports Illustrated* magazine. The following year, Fiedler won ten of the fifteen games he started for the Dolphins.

As Bob Griese did three decades ago, Jay Fiedler has shown that he can find a way to win. Superior intelligence and better-than-average mobility give him an edge over many quarterbacks with much stronger arms. Fiedler's intelligence shows in his ability to read defenses and make needed adjustments as a play develops. He seldom is fooled by shifting defenses, and, when his prime receiver is covered, he is quick enough to roam out of the pocket until a secondary receiver breaks free or to bootleg a first down when all else fails.

By varying his cadence and outsmarting his defenders with head fakes, Fiedler can often gain enough added time for his adequate arm strength and release to reach a receiver in stride on long post patterns; but pinpoint accuracy makes him particularly dangerous in making quick completions along the sidelines, especially when time is a factor.

Fiedler's quickness makes him unusually adept at avoiding sacks. His place in the All-Time Ranking of Great Jewish Athletes is projected on the likelihood that he achieves an All-Pro selection and either throws for or scores a Super Bowl touchdown, which would give him 7 points. He has the potential, however, to rank even higher.

NUMBER 47
LOU GORDON [6]

One-time college All-American Lou Gordon made a crucial fumble recovery for the winning Green Bay Packers in the 1936 National Football League Championship game. In a 1973 letter to

At 250 pounds, Lou Gordon was a large lineman by 1930 standards. (Photo courtesy of Lou Gordon.)

me, Gordon recalled some discrimination he experienced: "As a freshman football player at he University of Illinois, I encountered some prejudice. But, religion did not play a factor in my career." He added, "I was not necessarily aware of any special following from Jewish fans. I considered myself as an individual player and felt no obligation to stand up and act as a representative for the fans in matters of social interest."

NUMBER 48
MAX BAER [6]

In 1933, a boxer with a distant strain of Jewish heritage and the Mogen David on his trunks knocked out the hero of Nazi Germany—Max Schmeling, some three years before Schmeling would do the same to Joe Louis; but that night, Baer hurt Schmeling in round 10 with a hard right hand. Another right and, as Howard Cosell would later phrase it some forty years later, when Joe Frazier was losing his crown, "Down goes Schmeling! Down goes Schmeling! Down goes Schmeling!" Schmeling tried to get up but fell flat on his face and was counted out. The following year, Baer stunned the boxing world again with an eleventh-round knockout of the seemingly invincible six foot six inch and 260-pound Primo Carnera to win the World Heavyweight Championship.

NUMBER 49
HAROLD SOLOMON [5]

Tennis great Harold Solomon was not a power player. He relied instead on a tricky slice spin serve and precision lobs to keep his opponents off balance. His excellent ground strokes kept him ranked high in the top 10, and his gentlemanly demeanor made him a role model for young Jewish people. In a letter to me dated July 10, 1973, this is how he described his

Harold Solomon was one of the greatest clay court players in tennis history. (Photo courtesy of the United States Tennis Lawn Association, by Russ Adams.)

realization that he had a special Jewish following: "I have received many letters from Jewish people throughout the world. From those letters, I have come to realize that I do have a rather large following in the Jewish population—especially in Europe."

NUMBER 48
STEVE TANNEN [5]

One the great defensive backs in the National Football League when he was healthy, Steve Tannen drew a large Jewish following playing for the Jets in New York A high school track star turned poet, Tannen found his niche in the defensive backfield of the New York Jets. In addition to blazing speed, his fearless special team play earned him distinction as a feared tackler. Because

And it's picked off! Intercepted by Tannen! (Photo courtesy of the New York Jets.)

of the large concentration of Jews in New York, Tannen attracted a large Jewish following after being signed as a number one draft choice. Injuries curtailed his speed, but Tannen led the team in interceptions in 1972 with seven.

NUMBER 51
BRIAN GOTTFRIED [5]

Brian Gottfried was a hard-hitting tennis player who followed his serve to the net. He won many tournaments, but he was best known for two near misses: a semifinalist Wimbledon finish in 1980, which came four years after a near defeat of the legendary Bjorn Borg in the quarterfinal of the United States Open.

In a 1973 letter to me, Gottfried wrote:

> On the tennis circuit: there are so many different nationalities represented, it is impossible to keep track of who comes from where,

Brian Gottfried, a semifinalist Wimbledon finish in 1980. (Photo courtesy of the United States Tennis Lawn Association, by Russ Adams.)

much less everybody's religion. The only people who really dwell on a person's background are the press . . . . I am proud of my heritage. But, I want to become the best tennis player in the world regardless of race, nationality, or religion.

NUMBER 52
BRAD GILBERT [5]

Two of current tennis star Brad Gilbert's greatest achievements came in 1985 and 1986 with tournament championships in Tel Aviv, Israel. In January 1990, he was ranked fourth in the world. However, it was in 1987 that Gilbert scored his most symbolic triumphs as a Jewish athlete. That year, he helped the United States reach the World Team Cup finals in Dusseldorf, West Germany, and he scored three victories over German sports idol Boris Becker—a genuinely nice person; but because of Becker's national following, the victory made a statement to many Jewish people

It was not Brad Gilbert's tennis domination over German national hero Boris Becker that proved the Holocaust had failed but the fact that it was not widely regarded as significant. (Photo courtesy of ProServ, Inc., by Will Cofnuk.)

that the Holocaust had failed. The perennially top 10-ranked Gilbert also held victories over such tennis greats as Jimmy Connors and John McEnroe.

NUMBER 53
JULIE HELDMAN [5]

In 1969, Julie Heldman won the Italian Open. Heldman earned rankings high in the top ten until injuries put an abrupt end to her promising career. She gained prominence by wearing down Billie Jean King until she surrendered in a nationally televised match not long after King's stunning upset of Bobby Riggs in the much-heralded Battle of the Sexes. Heldman's use of the entire court also brought down such high-ranking players as Rosie Casals, Margaret Court, Chris Evert, Evonne Goolagong, Martina Navratilova, and Virginia Wade.

Julie Heldman's mother played at Wimbledon, but she made a name for herself by winning the Italian Open, ranking high in the top ten, and scoring a stunning upset victory over Billie Jean King. (Photo courtesy of the United States Tennis Lawn Association, by Russ Adams.)

NUMBER 54
AARON KRICKSTEIN [5]

At twenty-six, Aaron Krickstein won the Israel Tennis Center Classic in Tel Aviv in 1983 to become the youngest to win a Grand Prix tournament. Earlier that year, he had upset Vitas Gerulaitis in round 16 of the U.S. Open, at Flushing Meadow, New York, to become the youngest male to ever reach its fourth round and the youngest to obtain a top 10 ranking. It would be five years before Krickstein would again emerge as a dominant force in tennis. In the fourth round of the 1988 U.S. Open, former Wimbledon champion Stefan Edberg fell in defeat to Krickstein—who had fallen from number 7 in the world all the way to number 23 by then because of injuries.

Little did he know that nine years later in the fourth round of that same tournament, the U.S. Open, Krickstein would find the

After a spectacular run at the start of his career, Aaron Krickstein settled into a solid top 10 tennis player. (Photo courtesy of ProServ, Inc.)

crowd rooting against him. He faced Jimmy Connors in what the crowd realized was the last hurrah of Connors's vaunted double-backhand. Connors struggled to his last win.

NUMBER 55
ELIOT TELTSCHER [5]

Eliot Teltscher soared to number 6 in national tennis rankings in 1982. He earned his spot among the tennis elite by winning such tournaments as the Japan Open in Tokyo in 1983 and the Altech South African Open in Johannesburg in 1984. Like Brian Gottfried, Teltscher was best known for surprising high finishes in two tournaments that he did not win. Teltscher burst on the scene of professional tennis by losing to Vitas Gerulaitis in large part because of an infraction that he called on himself in 1978 and then upsetting John McEnroe in the second round of a Palm Springs tournament the following year. Teltscher defeated McEnroe at the Volvo

Eliot Teltscher lost a match to Vitas Gerulaitis in large part because of an infraction that he called on himself. (Photo courtesy of ProServ, Inc., by Carol Newsom.)

Masters in New York four years later. He also beat Jimmy Connors and Ivan Lendl during that period.

NUMBER 56
ELISE BURGIN [5]

As a four-time All-American at Stanford, Elise Burgin shared school honors during her college career with legendary football quarterback John Elway. In 1986, she won the Wild Dunes Invitational tennis tournament in Charleston. It was her first singles title in between such professional doubles championships as the 1987 Virginia Slims of New England, the 1986 Eckerd Open, and the 1986 Egbaston Classic with Ros Fairbank; the 1987 Virginia Slims of Washington with Pam Shriver; the 1986 European Open with B. Nagelson; the 1986 Virginia Slims of Houston with Martina Navratilova, where she also scored a finalist finish in singles play with victories over Manuela Maleeva and Zina Garrison; and the 1985 Virginia Slims of Indianapolis with Kathy Horvath. The *Baltimore Sun* described Burgin's tennis style as "serve and volley, serve and stay back; top spin, flat, slice."

Elise Burgin earned success as a left-handed tennis player who did the right thing. (Photo courtesy of Advantage International by Beverly Schafer)

NUMBER 57
JAY BERGER [5]

As a much-heralded former Clemson University All-American, Jay Berger emerged in 1986 as champion of the USTA Satellite in West Palm Beach and the Buenos Aires Grand Prix. By 1990, he had a top ten ranking. With a style that put a premium of accuracy over power, in 1990 Berger joined Brad Gilbert and Aaron Krickstein in the top 10 of the tennis world. It was the only time that many Jewish players have been ranked that high simultaneously. One of the top clay court players, Berger kept opponents off balance in a style similar to that of Harold Solomon.

Berger used pinpoint accuracy to keep opponents off balance (Photo courtesy of ProServ, Inc.)

NUMBER 58
TOM OKKER [5]

Tom Okker reportedly went "out of his way" to publicly identify himself as having pride in his father's Judaism. Okker won the 1968 and 1969 South African Title and finished as a finalist in the 1968 United States Open. In the late 1970s, he reached the semifinals and quarterfinals at Wimbledon in successive years; and as a doubles partner, he won the United States, Italian, and French Opens.

NUMBER 59
LARRY SHERRY [4]

In 1959, Larry Sherry became the first relief pitcher to be named World Series Most Valuable Player by winning two games and

Larry Sherry overcame the disability of being born with two deformed feet to become one of the first star relief pitchers in baseball history. (Photo courtesy of the Los Angeles Dodgers.)

saving the other two after winning, as a rookie, a playoff game that lifted the Dodgers into the World Series. During the regular season that year, Sherry had compiled a pitching record worthy of Rookie of the Year consideration. With nearly twice as many strikeouts as walks, he won seven games against two losses with a stunning earned run average of only 2.19. Although he won fourteen games in 1960, Sherry would never regain that form again.

If only for a year, the emergence of Sherry as a star in a relief role made him a pioneer—for people with disabilities because of his two deformed feet and because relief pitchers took second billing to starters then. Sherry was one of the first relief specialists not originally groomed to be a starter. Whatever made Sherry dominating for a year and why will never be known; but some time during the course of it, baseball changed forever. He changed the way that relief pitchers are valued.

NUMBER 60
GOODY ROSEN [4]

Goody Rosen earned All-Star distinction in 1945 when he hit .325 with 12 home runs. A spray hitter to all fields, Rosen hit .281 in 1938 and 1946. However, it was with his glove that Goody Rosen earned distinction. A great fielding center fielder, his style of play would be adapted by many legends who followed.

Rosen introduced the style of playing shallow that would be adapted by many great center fielders who came after him. In the 1950s, Red Sox center fielder Jimmy Piersall was often compared to Rosen.

By instinctively darting backward at the crack of the bat, Rosen made circus catches with his back to the plate—much like the historic catch off the bat of Vic Wertz made by Willie Mays in the 1954 World Series.

Early in his career, Rosen had weakness in the field on shallow balls looped into short center because of his tendency to anticipate balls being hit over his head. He occasionally would react late and then would occasionally overrun the ball in a desperate attempt to make up for the lost time.

As good as Rosen became in the outfield, many believed that he belonged at shortstop—a position then that did not require power hitting of its incumbent, as did center field.

Rosen's skills were similar to those of Lou Boudreau, who came into the major leagues around the same time. If their roles had been reversed, it may have been Rosen rather than Boudreau who made the National Baseball Hall of Fame.

NUMBER 61
SONNY HERTZBERG [4]

Basketball guard Sonny Hertzberg was captain and high scorer of first the New York Knicks and then the Boston Celtics. Hertzberg described himself for me as having been "an accu-

Sonny Hertzberg was captain and high scorer of the original Knickerbockers and Washington Capitols teams. (Photo courtesy of Sonny Hertzberg.)

rate shooter, play developer, and strategist." He also gained a reputation for playing tough defense. At five feet ten inches, he could guard the opponent's primary shooter. He was also quick enough to press the ball while it was being brought in by the opposing point guard. His standing set shot was ideally suited for the half-court strategies that were typically played in that era.

NUMBER 62
MARK CLEAR [4]

A two-time American League All-Star, Mark Clear maintained an awesome pace of nearly a strikeout per inning pitched as a dominating relief pitcher over the course of his career. With the California Angels, he averaged eleven wins per year; and with the Boston Red Sox, he peaked with fourteen wins in the 1982 campaign. He struck out more batters than hits allowed nine different years.

Mark Clear compiled a record with three teams that compares favorably with many of the most prominent relief pitchers ever to play the game. (Photo courtesy of the Milwaukee Brewers.)

NUMBER 63
LENNY ROSENBLUTH [4]

In 1957, two-time All-America basketball star Lenny Rosenbluth led the University of North Carolina to the National Collegiate Athletic Association title over legendary Wilt Chamberlain's Kansas team. Rosenbluth outscored not only Chamberlain but all of the other players in that tournament as well. During the regular 1956–1957 season, the six foot five inch Rosenbluth averaged nearly 28 points per game for a North Carolina team that had a run of thirty-two consecutive wins. He played briefly for the Philadelphia Warriors in the National Basketball Association.

At the University of Missouri, Brad Edelman was an Honorable Mention All-American. (Photo courtesy of the University of Missouri.)

NUMBER 64
BRAD EDELMAN [4]

In college, Brad Edelman played as an interior offensive lineman and as the snapper for both punting and kicking. He was drafted in the second round by the New Orleans Saints in 1982 and selected to the Pro Bowl six years later. He retired from football after the following season. Edelman had earned a reputation throughout the National Football League as one of the great blockers of his era for the run.

NUMBER 65
RICHIE SCHEINBLUM [4]

When Richie Scheinblum joined a team, it was never a good idea for him to send out his laundry. He was often traded. But 1972 saw Richie Scheinblum make the American League All-Star team for leading the league in hitting for most of the season. This was how

Against southpaws, the switch-hitting Scheinblum swung from the right side; against righties, from the left. (Photo courtesy of the Kansas City Royals.)

Scheinblum recalled for me the effect that being a famous Jewish athlete had on him when eleven Jewish athletes were murdered in Munich:

> I feel I have a Jewish following and I feel representative of a lot of people. . . . I wore the emblematic black band . . . not only because they were Jewish athletes, but because they were human beings. I made some of my feelings known in print and did afterwards feel there would be a threatening response. But, nothing was said.

NUMBER 66
JASON MARQUIS
[4 PROJECTED]

A speed of better than ninety-four miles per hour gives Jason Marquis outstanding potential, but the question facing every hard throwing young Major League Baseball pitcher with occasional control problems is whether letting up on a fastball to increase command of it would make his other pitches easier to hit. Assuming that Marquis finds the right balance between speed and control, it is reasonable to project his ranking on the basis of 4 ranking points on the premise that he is likely to achieve either four years of fifteen to eighteen wins with a 3.10 or higher earned run average or two fifteen-win seasons and a World Series pitching win.

NUMBER 67

GABE KAPLER [4, PROJECTED]

Some fifty-nine years after Joe DiMaggio had set what many sports fans still consider to be the greatest of sports records by hitting safely in fifty-six straight 1941 games, a then twenty-five-year-old Jewish outfielder accomplished the first leg of it. Gabe Kapler had base hits in twenty-eight straight games for the Texas Rangers on his way to a .302 batting average in 2000. Kapler is ranked on the basis of his achieving 4 projected points from the probability of his hitting between .300 and .339

Gabe Kapler could the strongest contact hitter in the major leagues. With a change in his swing, he has the strength to immediately become a significant slugger with power to all fields. (Photo courtesy of the Texas Rangers.)

with less than 25 home runs one more time. On the basis of the explosive power Kapler exhibited in the minor leagues by slugging 28 homers and setting a Southern League record for runs batted in with 146, Kapler could ultimately rank much higher.

NUMBER 68
MIKE ROSSMAN [3]

In its review of *The Jewish Athletes' Hall of Fame*, the *National Jewish Post and Opinion* reported that former World Boxing Association light heavyweight boxing champion Mike Rossman "long ago admitted that he was a Catholic." At issue was my inclusion

When Mike Rossman boxed with the Star of David on his trunks, memories were rekindled of the long line of Jewish champions. (Photo courtesy of Capital Center.)

of Rossman, who still qualifies here on the basis of his Jewish mother. The religious practice of any Jewish athlete is only conjecture, particularly in this era of assimilation. Rossman won the World Boxing Association Light Heavyweight Boxing Championship in 1978 under his mother's Jewish name, and he fought with the Star of David on his trunks as "The Jewish Bomber." After an appearance in New York's fabled Madison Square Garden, a mob of Jewish youths in yarmulkes gave him two unheard-of standing ovations and stormed his victorious locker room after the match. In 1974, I asked Rossman whether he would have liked to have somehow fought Adolf Hitler's sports idol Max Schmeling. "I am glad I was not around to meet Max Schmeling; for today, I would be an old man."

NUMBER 69
ROBY YOUNG [3]

In the 1970s, the New York Cosmos's Roby Young emerged as the greatest Jewish soccer play of all time. Before playing soccer in

Although soccer was just emerging as an American sport, Roby Young attracted a huge Jewish following as a member of a New York team. (Photo courtesy of the New York Cosmos, by Paul Bereswill.)

the United States, Young had been captain of the Israeli national team. In a 1974 letter to me, he wrote, "Any image of an unathletic Jew . . . no longer exists . . . because of the influence of the State of Israel, with its young and strong generation. . . . I wish I could live to see a world without politics; I'd like a world of sports."

NUMBER 70
MIKE EPSTEIN [3]

Awesome size and minor league heroics earned Mike Epstein the nickname "Super Jew" before he reached the major leagues. After a spectacular minor league career, Epstein hit 30 home runs for the 1969 Washington Senators under the tutelage of manager Ted Williams and 26 for the 1972 World Champion Oakland A's—when he joined Ken Holtzman in risking his life to play with a black armband in protest of the murders of Jewish athletes at the Munich Olympics that year—but he never came close to achieving the greatness expected of him as a player.

Mike Epstein swings. Poor eyesight hampered his hitting and prevented him from maintaining a respectable batting average, but this one was gone. (Photo courtesy of the California Angels.)

In the 1984 Los Angeles Olympics, Mitch Gaylord showed unparalleled precision on the parallel bars, an eloquent grace on the horse vault, and brute force on the rings. (Photo courtesy of the United States Gymnastics Federation.)

NUMBER 71
MITCH GAYLORD [3]

By terming part of his spectacular routine a so-called Gaylord flip, Mitch Gaylord earned well-deserved distinction as an innovator in gymnastics in addition to the respect he commanded by winning four medals at a single Olympiad. At the 1984 Los Angeles Olympics, Gaylord won the gold medal for team gymnastics, a silver medal in vaulting, and bronze medals for both the rings and the parallel bars.

NUMBER 72
BARRY ASHER [3]

As "Best Dressed Bowler," an unusually deep drop of his right knee somehow enabled Barry Asher to unleash a rapid rolling

Barry Asher became the second Jewish bowler, after Mark Roth, to gain entrance into the Professional Bowler's Association Hall of Fame. (Photo courtesy of the Professional Bowler's Association.)

ball with an exceedingly fashionable look. Asher's unique bowling style enabled him to average a score of 247 over a forty-two-game span. In 1976, Asher became only the fifteenth bowler to win ten Professional Bowler's Association titles. Asher bowled three perfect 300 games and once beat the legendary Jewish bowler, Mark Roth.

NUMBER 73
MARSHALL HOLMAN [3]

Marshall Holman launched one of the most successful career turnarounds in bowling history by winning the 1986 Firestone Tournament of Champions a decade after capturing the same

Marshall Holman played in the shadow of Mark Roth, who looks like Babe Ruth; Holman does not look like Lou Gehrig. (Photo courtesy of the Professional Bowler's Association.)

prestigious bowling tournament. The following year, he was named Professional Bowler's Association Player of the Year with a performance so consistent that he was able to capture the coveted award without winning a single tournament. The most dramatic moment in Holman's career came in 1984 when he bowled 280 to defeat legendary Mark Roth at the Brunswick Memorial World Open.

NUMBER 74
MARILYN RAMENOFSKY [3]

In a 1973 letter to me, International Swimming Hall of Fame director Buck Dawson described Marilyn Ramenofsky as "the first female to swim a perfect freestyle stroke." Ramenofsky won a 1964 swimming silver Olympic medal as a three-time world record holder.

In several 1974 and 1975 letters to me, Ramenofsky shared these thoughts:

In retrospect, I feel there was some prejudice shown against me by the U.S. Olympic Women's swimming coach and some preference was given to other swimmers on the team. Whether that was because I was Jewish, I cannot directly relate.

I have always felt that the Jewish community has backed my efforts and—as my career progressed—so did my Jewish following.

Beginning in 1961, my family and the Phoenix Jewish community provided a great deal of spiritual support and helped raise travel money for my first international swimming competition as a member of the U.S. Maccabiah Team in Israel.

In 1964, as the only Jewish woman on the U.S. Women's Olympic Swimming Team and a world record holder, I felt a strong Jewish sentiment both at home and abroad. The Jewish recognition was culminated for me upon my return to Israel for the 1965 Maccabiah Games. I was applauded as a champion by my competitors, by my teammates and by the people of Israel—what a wonderful memory!

The great interest in and commitment to striving athletics stems from the pride Jews feel and place upon achievement in any field. . . . I dislike the misuse of privileges and recognition that success in

Marilyn Ramenofsky was the greatest female Jewish swimmer of all time. (Photo courtesy of Marilyn Ramenofsky.)

any endeavor provides for the promotion of selfish intentions. It is wrong to utilize athletic success as a stepping stone for political or theatrical careers. Each endeavor demands merit in its own right.

While I was intensely training, I had very little time for extra things. The devotion to my sport was total. As a high school student, my life was filled with five to six hours of training a day, competition, and studies. In a very real sense, the world-class athlete lives in a vacuum.

NUMBER 75

BARRY LATMAN [2]

Barry Latman's best year as a Major League Baseball pitcher came with the Cleveland Indians, in 1961, when he went thirteen and five and made the American League All-Star team. He is best remembered, however, by having been traded even up for Herb Score—almost a Sandy Koufax clone whose brilliance was obliterated by a blast off the bat of New York Yankee Gil Mc-Dougald—after one of the most horrifying moments in baseball

Barry Latman was reported to be one of the most religious Jewish pitchers ever to play the game. (Photo courtesy of the Cleveland Indians.)

history. Score hurt his arm in a comeback attempt. In Latman, the Indians opted for a healthier armed pitcher—but one with a less blazing fast ball and control problems that he never would master. Latman was a devoutly religious Jew.

NUMBER 76
MIKE HARTMAN [2]

Left wing Mike Hartman played nine of his thirteen-season professional hockey career in the National Hockey League with the Buffalo Sabres, Winnipeg Jets, Tampa Bay Lightning, and New York Rangers. Although he played with the Sabres the longest, Hartman may be best remembered as the enforcer for the 1994 New York Ranger Stanley Cup championship team because of his rugged style and reputation as a banger. Although Hartman frequently engaged in fights, he never made a blind-side hit or otherwise endangered an opponent's career. Hartman intimidated

Mike Hartman holds on to the Stanley Cup after helping the New York Rangers win it. (Photo courtesy of the New York Rangers.)

opponents within the rules of the game, much like a baseball pitcher who throws high and inside but seldom hits anyone.

NUMBER 77
JOHN FRANK [2]

A number two draft choice out of Mount Lebanon High School in Pittsburgh and Ohio State University, John Frank demonstrated his importance as a tight end to the San Francisco 49ers in the phenomenal difference between the team's winning percentage with him in and out of the lineup. An early retirement did not erase the memory of mental intensity and aggressive physical play that earned Frank selections on two "All-Madden" mythical teams announced annually by the former coach turned commentator John Madden.

The fame and fortune of football was just not worth Frank bypassing what he wanted in life. He retired early to complete medical school.

Quarterback Joe Montana considered tight end John Frank one of his most reliable receivers on the San Francisco 49ers football dynasty. (Photo courtesy of the San Francisco 49ers.)

NUMBER 78
PAUL WEINTRAUB [2]

Phil Weintraub was a .300-hitting center fielder for the New York Giants with an enormous Jewish following. Weintraub did not lose his stroke during his years away from the game for World War II military service. He hit .311 in 1938 and .311 in 1944, his first year back. Although Weintraub never hit more than 13 home runs in an entire season, he once drove in 11 runs in a single game.

NUMBER 79
ART SHAMSKY [2]

After hitting .300 during the regular season, Shamsky hit an astronomical .538 in the championship series to get the 1969 World Champion New York Miracle Mets into that World Series. But his

Chronic back miseries cut short Art Shamsky's career. (Photo courtesy of the New York Mets.)

greatest personal accomplishment came on August 12, 1966. Shamsky entered a thirteen-inning game as a pinch hitter and homered. He stayed in the game and hit two more. Two days later, again as a pinch hitter, he hit his fourth consecutive homer. He had tied a record.

NUMBER 80
MORRIE ARNOVICH [2]

Outfielder Morrie Arnovich was brought in to temporarily fill a vacancy created at the Polo Grounds in New York when Phil Weintraub left the Giants for military service during World War II. Arnovich earned an All-Star berth and a place in *The All-Time Ranking of Great Jewish Athletes* by hitting .324 in 1939.

NUMBER 81
ELLIOTT MADDOX [2]

Elliott Maddox is the only one included in *The All-Time Rankings of Great Jewish Athletes* who converted into the religion. Maddox hit .303 in 1974 for the New York Yankees after converting. I interviewed him in 1988. This is what he told me:

> I definitely considered myself as Jewish during my playing days and formally converted to the religion in 1975. However, I did not notice a special interest in my career by Jewish fans probably because my being Jewish was not the most obvious thing about my appearance. I did not marry someone Jewish; but I still practice Judaism.

Maddox was a member of the New York Yankee team that included Ken Holtzman. Maddox acknowledged to me that the psychological letdown from two years of inactivity did ruin Holtzman's career. "His arm was healthy and he may have been headed to the Hall of Fame; for whatever reason, Billy Martin refused to use him," Maddox said.

NUMBER 82
RON BLOMBERG [2]

Ron Blomberg had one of the sweetest swings in baseball against right-handers and maintained a better than .300 average against them. He would often pause to watch a slicing hit bounce to the wall. Blomberg tended to bail out against southpaws. When the American League instituted the designated hitter, Blomberg became the first player to assume that role.

For clinicians, this photograph could serve as the ultimate "Thematic Apperception Test." Depending on various factors, Ron Blomberg might be perceived as following through on a line drive up the alley, preparing to slam his bat to the ground after a strikeout, or merely finishing a practice swing for the photographer. (Photo courtesy of the New York Yankees.)

Shep Messing demonstrates what they did teach him at Harvard. (Photo courtesy of the New York Cosmos.)

NUMBER 83
SHEP MESSING [2]

A participant of the 1972 Munich Olympics, two-time Harvard All-American soccer goalie Shep Messing had been Most Valuable Player of the National Collegiate Athletic Association finals the previous year. After the Olympics, Messing joined the New York Cosmos and excited his Jewish following with many spectacular saves.

NUMBER 84
BO BELINSKY [2]

Southpaw pitcher Bo Belinsky was the son of a Jewish mother and Polish Gentile who, after his career, would become one himself. He drew press attention as a rookie by pitching a no-hitter and going on to date Mamie Van Doren, Tina Louise, and Ann Margaret. He married Playboy Playmate of the Year Jo Collins, but he won fewer than thirty games over a nine-year career and lost nearly twice as many. In promotional materials for his book, *Bo: Pitching and Wooing* with Maury Allen (Dial, 1973), Belinsky was quoted as saying, "I don't feel sorry for myself; I've been in the sun." He received more mileage out of a no-hitter than any pitcher in history.

Bo Belinsky shows the form that enabled him to pitch a no-hitter as a rookie. (Photo courtesy of the California Angels.)

NUMBER 85
SCOTT SCHOENEWEIS
[2, PROJECTED]

If resiliency is the requirement for Scott Schoeneweis to achieve a fifteen-game win or fifty-save season, he has already demonstrated that quality twice. On his way to the major leagues, Schoeneweis overcame two obstacles—cancer and reconstructive elbow surgery at Duke University—to resume his role as ace of the Blue Devil's staff and later emerge as a left-handed starting pitcher in the majors. With the Anaheim Angels, Schoeneweis has put together stretches of brilliant pitching against some of the most formidable big league teams. In both 2000 and 2002, he won four games in a row as a starter by maintaining movement of his vaunted sinker ball; but his best success may have been achieved in the bullpen where he began to show promise as a reliever. As he approaches thirty, his stretches of brilliance and intestinal fortitude warrant a ranking based on a projection of two years of fifteen to eighteen wins with a 3.10 or higher earned run average or a year with forty to fifty-four games saved if he remains a reliever.

NUMBER 86
ERNIE GRUNFELD [1]

During the seventies, Ernie Grunfeld closed out his National Basketball Association career with the New York Knicks as an

At the University of Tennessee, Ernie Grunfeld made Scholastic Coach first team All America— that after being the first high schooler to make the United States basketball team for the Maccabiah Games. (Photo courtesy of the University of Tennessee.)

unheralded but valued role player. In college at the University of Tennessee, he had provided rugged rebounding and inside scoring when he wasn't setting picks for Bernard King—an excellent scorer who would be reunited with Grunfeld in New York. After his playing days, Grunfeld became a general manager.

NUMBER 87
ALBERT SCHWARTZ [1]

In 1930, Albert Schwartz became a National Collegiate Athletic Association triple crown winner in freestyle swimming. Two years later, he won an Olympic bronze medal in the 100-yard freestyle swimming. Had Schwartz competed during the following Olympiad in Berlin, he would have performed in the presence of Hitler.

The anguish of training and the pressure of competition appeared to be evident in Albert Schwartz's eyes. (Photo courtesy of the International Swimming Hall of Fame.)

In 1972, Donald Cohan was the first Jew to make the U.S. Olympic yachting team. (Photo courtesy of Donald Cohan.)

NUMBER 88
DONALD COHAN [1]

Olympic yachting bronze medalist Donald Cohan had to be tough. He competed in the 1972 Olympiad against men half his age. In a 1987 letter to me, Cohan displayed his Harvard Law eloquence in this way: "The last official act of [expletives deleted] Avery Brundage was to hang an Olympic medal around my neck." Cohan then explained whether being Jewish caused him to have a different attitude toward his competitive approach: "Frankly, I think it does; and although I'm quite competitive to start with, there is always that little tug in the back of my mind that drives me to be the last one to throw in the towel." Cohan saw this as an advantage. "At times, I think this puts extra pressure on me . . . knowing that being Jewish requires me to hold to the highest of standards." But then he added, "I don't think this is a burden; and I think, in the long run, [it] has been a very good guide and anchor for me."

BRENT NOVOSELSKY [0]

Known in the trenches for his durability, Brent Novoselsky was unusual in a game prolific with injuries. Over the course of his seven-year career, he seldom missed a game despite his penchant

Quarterback Jim McMahon credited much of his success with both the Chicago Bears and Minnesota Vikings to the blocking and pass catching of his tight end, Brent Novoselsky. Here, he makes a great diving catch. (Photo courtesy of the Minnesota Vikings.)

for bruising blocks and bone-crushing special team tackles. During one stretch, Novoselsky played in sixty-six straight games at tight end or on special teams.

NUMBER 90
ANDY COHEN [0]

Andy Cohen was not the first Jewish player; but there was enormous pressure put on him when he played better than expected after succeeding Frankie Frisch and Rogers Hornsby at second base for the New York Giants. In the opening game of the 1928 season, Cohen outplayed Hornsby in winning the game for New York. That created an overwhelming following from New York's large Jewish population. When Cohen's unexpected hot hitting won the following Sunday's game, Jewish fans mobbed Cohen

Andy Cohen played a similar role for Jewish people that Jackie Robinson later did for blacks. (Photo courtesy of Andy Cohen.)

and carried him off the field. In a September 12, 1935, *Sporting News* article, Frederick G. Lieb reported that "Jewish admirers besieged his house, camped there day and night to get a peek at Andy." Cohen had compiled a respectable .281 batting average; but within a year the pressure proved too much to bear, and he retired.

I posed questions to Cohen's brother, Sid, who is best remembered as the pitcher who surrendered Babe Ruth's last American League home run. This was how Sid replied:

> Neither my brother Andy nor I ever played ball on either Rosh Hashanah or Yom Kippur. Our wonderful mother told us people would have more respect for Jews by our not working on these special days. . . . Greenberg, Koufax, Holtzman and all the rest [later] sat in the Synagogue and prayed.

In a letter from Andy Cohen to me in 1973, he wrote:

> The label "Great Jewish Hope" did inflict pressure. It did seem to spur me on, but as I look back:
> There were times I tried too hard. I certainly was aware of a special following from Jewish fans; I guess I considered myself a representative of these people.
> I encountered prejudice from players as well as fans. The tremendous publicity and the fact I played so well in my first game helped cause the prejudice.
> But I had true friends in my manager, most of my teammates, several umpires, and some of the reporters covering the club. Much of the publicity created good will.
> For the first time in its history, *Fourants*—the well-known Jewish paper—ran box scores of New York Giant baseball games. After an off day at the Polo Grounds, the *Fourants* ran a banner on its front page that read" "No Game Today: Andy Must Be Sick."
> Many of the Jewish fans who came to the Polo Grounds for the first time asked what kind of seats were available.
> Ticket sellers would offer them box seats behind first or third base. Some of these fans would insist on box seats behind second base.
> All of the New York papers ran humorous cartoons about me. My favorite showed a Jewish mother urging her son to eat a certain brand of soup to "grow up to be like Andy C."

NUMBER 91
BRAD AUSMUS [0]

Catcher Brad Ausmus tied a record in 2002 for hitting into the most double plays in a season. Ausmus has the Ivy League education, preppie look, and articulate manner of an athlete destined for politics. Yet he seems almost impossible to knock off his feet no matter how many times he is smashed with a foul tip run into by an opponent attempting to score. While not a slugger, Ausmus maintains a high enough batting average to complement a defensive talent that inevitably finds itself on some team's starting lineup.

NUMBER 92
DANNY SCHAYES [0]

By the time Dolph Schayes's son, Danny, landed on his eighth team, he was the longest tenured player in the National Basket-

Pitted against irreverent rebounding king Dennis Rodman before Rodman dyed his hair and went on to become a tattooed cult hero, journeyman center Danny Schayes fakes him off his feet before going up again to score. (Photo courtesy of the Denver Nuggets.)

ball Association. Schayes pulled down 18 rebounds for the Utah Jazz against the Houston Rockets in 1982 and, seven years later, scored 37 points against them.

NUMBER 93
SCOTT RADINSKY [0]

A singer and drummer of punk-rock bands Pulley and Scared Straight, southpaw reliever Scott Radinsky made a successful comeback from Hodgkin's disease while pitching for the Chicago White Sox in 1994 and continued as one of baseball's premier middle relievers. Of the four teams for which he played, the Los Angeles Dodgers benefited most from his pitching. While with the Dodgers, Radinsky joined the band Pulley. He recorded not only more music but a baseball record of three consecutive years with earned run averages of less than 3 runs per game.

As a member of a popular hard-rock group, former star relief pitcher Scott Radinsky followed the long line of artistic and scholarly Jewish people who succeed in sports because of their brilliance. (Photo courtesy of the Los Angeles Dodgers.)

NUMBER 94
AL LEVINE [0]

Al Levine played minor league baseball with Michael Jordan, but unlike the great basketball star, he has gone on to have a successful major league career. Levine has established himself as the ultimate middle reliever. A current right-handed pitcher often used in middle-inning relief, Levine shows versatility that enables him also to serve as a closer or periodic starter. He effectively mixes a sinker and hard slider to give the illusion of added velocity to his more-than-adequate fastball. His consistency is reflected in a distinct pattern of comparatively low earned run averages for his high-scoring era. He is most effective against right-handed hitters, which accounts for the majority of batters and makes him ideal for spot use. His ability to pitch with minimal rest enables him to be used in approximately a third of his team's games.

NUMBER 95
RONNIE STERN [0]

A synonym for *harsh* or *severe* was a fitting name for John Stern because of his rough style of hockey. Selected as an underage junior by the Vancouver Canucks as the seventieth overall pick in the fourth round of the 1986 National Hockey League draft, Ronnie Stern invariably found himself among National Hockey League leaders in penalty minutes over the often-turbulent course of a thirteen-year career. At six feet and more than two hundred pounds, Stern was called a thug by critics but a hero by his fans. When opposing teams would rally, he would be called in to stop the momentum by starting a fight. Eventually, Stern's mere presence on the ice would have nearly the same effect. He played right wing for the Vancouver Canucks, the Calgary Flames, and the San Diego Sharks before retiring at the end of the 1999–2000 season.

NUMBER 96
BRUCE MESNER [0]

In 1987, nose tackle Bruce Mesner made one of that year's most dramatic defensive plays for his Buffalo Bills when he batted down a Warren Moon pass on a key defensive stand late in a game in which Buffalo rallied to win, but it was as an All-America Honorable Mention collegiate at the University of Maryland where he took a more memorable stand. Mesner and fellow Jewish player Neal Sampson missed Maryland's game against Penn State because it fell on the Jewish High Holy Day, Yom Kippur, despite pressure from coach Bobby Ross to play. "But, it helped me respect Coach Ross more as a person because he didn't say, 'OK,' and hold a grudge; or say, 'OK,' and not find out any more about something that was so important to us," Mesner was quoted in the *Washington Post* as saying.

Bruce Mesner made headlines by not playing football on a Jewish holiday. (Photo courtesy of the University of Maryland.)

Joel Kramer was undersized as a center. He made up for his lack of bulk with intelligence—knowing where to position himself in anticipation of where a rebound might land. (Photo courtesy of the Phoenix Suns.)

NUMBER 97
JOEL KRAMER [0]

On prime-time television, Joel Kramer made a mark in the National Basketball Association as a tenacious rebounder—a skill he mastered with an uncanny ability to establish floor position near where the ball would come down.

Kramer played five years at center for the Phoenix Suns. As a rookie in the Western Conference Finals of the National Basketball Association playoffs in 1979, Kramer came off the bench to replace injured star center Alvin Adams. Kramer led the Suns to three straight wins, including one in which he scored 19 points.

NUMBER 98
ROSS BROOKS [0]

During the 1972–1973 hockey season, Brooks maintained a goals against average of 2.38 per game for the Boston Braves of

Ross Brooks—the first Jewish goalie in the National Hockey League. (Photo courtesy of the Boston Bruins.)

the American Hockey League. That enabled him to join the Boston Bruins of the National Hockey League, where he remained for the three following seasons. That could have been the perfect climax to a professional career that spanned twenty years, but Brooks returned for one more year in the American Hockey League for the Rochester Americans. Although his only National Hockey League playoff appearance for the Bruins saw him give up three goals in twenty minutes, Brooks's competent play as goalie earned him a Jewish following and an enduring reputation for toughness among all fans of the game. With the exception of professional boxing, the position of hockey goalie may be the most punishing in sports. In becoming the first Jewish goalie in professional hockey history, Brooks drew acclaim with an unbeaten stretch of thirteen games.

NUMBER 99
ALAN VEINGRAD [0]

In 1990, a blurb in the *Washington Post* read, "Green Bay's Tony Mandrich, the number two pick in the entire [National Football League] draft, on not being able to beat out Alan Veingrad, a free agent from East Texas State: 'I go home at night sometimes and pound my head against the wall, I'm so frustrated.'"

That report came after Mandrich had been widely rumored to be in line for a shot in boxing against then-undefeated Mike Tyson for the World Heavyweight Championship.

Veingrad ended his brief career as an offensive lineman after a stint on a Dallas Cowboys World Champion team. However, it was in the Sunday, January 22, 1995, edition of *The New York Times* that Veingrad made his mark on the National Football League with a guest editorial. Veingrad revealed incidents of

Alan Veingrad made the National Football League despite not being drafted and then being cut by two teams. (Photo courtesy of the Green Bay Packers.)

proselytizing by players at East Texas State University whose delusion that the United States is allegedly a Christian country resulted in them trying to convert him away from Judaism.

"Sitting through team prayer meetings before the games . . . I retained a strong sense of Jewish dignity and pride," Veingrad recalled. Later with the Green Bay Packers, Veingrad wrote how "at pre-game prayer sessions, when my teammates would join hands and recite the Lord's Prayer, I would say my own silent prayer, a Jewish prayer," he added. Unlike many contemporary Jews, including prominent Jewish athletes, Veingrad wrote that he married "a Jewish woman with whom I could share my love for Judaism and build a Jewish family."

NUMBER 100
PETER REVSON [0]

Peter Revson, whose father was Jewish, was proud of that heritage. In a 1973 letter to me, he had this to say about it: "My

Peter Revson was proud of his father's Jewish heritage. (Photo courtesy of Indianapolis Motor Speedway Corporation.)

mother is a WASP. But, being half-Jewish, I am very sympathetic and understanding of Jewish problems."

I asked Revson whether he had ever encountered prejudice because of his ethnic background. "If I do encounter it, I put myself in a position where I don't have to tolerate it," he replied.

Revson was so gifted that he nearly won the first Super Star Sports Tournament against professional athletes from all major sports. In 1971, he had won the pole position in the Indianapolis 500 for U.S. Auto Club Championship cars with a record 178.696 miles per hour and finished as the runner-up.

In 1974, Revson was romantically linked with the Miss World at the time. He was described as "the leading road racing driver in the United States and one of the foremost drivers in the world" in a wire release from United Press International on March 22 of that year. On that day, his car crashed and he died.

Chapter 4

All-Time Rankings by Era

Rankings for 1985–Present

1. Shawn Green [50, projected]
2. Harris Barton [28, projected]
3. Amy Alcott [21]
4. Corey Pavin [21]
5. Kenny Bernstein [12]
6. Mathieu Schneider [11, projected]
7. Mark Roth [9]
8. Jay Fiedler [7, projected]
9. Brad Gilbert [5]
10. Jay Berger [5]
11. Brad Edelman [4]
12. Jason Marquis [4, projected]
13. Gabe Kapler [4, projected]
14. Marshall Holman [3]
15. Mike Hartman [2]
16. Scott Schoeneweis [2, projected]
17. Brent Novoselsky [0]
18. Brad Ausmus [0]
19. Danny Schayes [0]
20. Scott Radinsky [0]
21. Al Levine [0]
22. Ronnie Stern [0]
23. Bruce Mesner [0]
24. Alan Veingrad [0]

Rankings for 1970–1984

1. Ken Holtzman [46, projected]
2. Lyle Alzado [20]
3. Nancy Lieberman [17]
4. Ed Newman [15]
5. Mark Spitz [14]
6. Randy Grossman [11]
7. Neal Walk [7]
8. Steve Stone [7]
9. Harold Solomon [5]
10. Steve Tannen [5]
11. Brian Gottfried [5]
12. Mitch Gaylord [3]
13. Barry Asher [3]
14. John Frank [2]
15. Elliott Maddox [2]
16. Ron Blomberg [2]
17. Shep Messing [2]
18. Ernie Grunfeld [1]
19. Donald Cohan [1]
20. Joel Kramer [0]
21. Ross Brooks [0]
22. Peter Revson [0]

Rankings for 1955–1969

1. Sandy Koufax [78]
2. Dolph Schayes [57]
3. Ron Mix [51]
4. Rudy LaRusso [16]
5. Issac Berger [13]
6. Art Heyman [7]
7. Tom Okker [5]
8. Larry Sherry [4]
9. Lenny Rosenbluth [4]
10. Marilyn Ramenofsky [3]
11. Barry Latman [2]
12. Bo Belinsksy [2]

Rankings for 1940–1954

1. Sid Luckman [65]
2. Dick Savitt [41, projected]
3. Lou Boudreau [37]
4. Al Rosen [25]
5. Marshall Goldberg [22]
6. Max Zaslofsky [18, projected]
7. Sid Gordon [10]
8. Henry Wittenberg [10
9. Goody Rosen [4]
10. Sonny Hertzberg [4]

Rankings for 1925–1939

1. Hank Greenberg [80]
2. Benny Friedman [39, projected]
3. Buddy Myer [34, projected]
4. Barney Ross [32]
5. Maxie Rosenbloom [20]
6. Harry Newman [17]
7. Louis "Kid" Kaplan [17]
8. Harry Danning [10]
9. Lou Gordon [6]
10. Max Baer [6]
11. Paul Weintraub [2]
12. Morrie Arnovich [2]
13. Albert Schwartz [1]
14. Andy Cohen [0]

Rankings for 1900–1924

1. Benny Leonard [49]
2. Nat Holman [30]
3. Battling Levinsky [27]
4. Ted "Kid" Lewis [22]
5. Abe Attell [19]
6. Jackie Fields [17]
7. Erskine Mayer [8]
8. Lew Tendler [7]

Chapter 5

Unsung Jewish Athletes

The earliest baseball player to whom I posed questions was Al Schacht, who had gained fame that far exceeded his accomplishments as a pitcher. Schacht was known as "The Clown Prince of Baseball" for his comedy routines.

In 1974, I received a letter from Schacht reflecting on his career. This is how he remembered it:

> My first engagement as an entertainer in baseball came in 1921, in the World Series between the Yankees and Giants at the Polo Grounds. The show consisted of about 20 minutes of pantomime . . . before the game started. In all: I entertained in 25 different World Series and 15 All Star games.

Schacht's career as a pitcher was very brief, but even the greatest of Jewish baseball players had somewhat brief careers compared to other legends of the game. The thirteen years broken up by military service of Hank Greenberg and twelve years played by Sandy Koufax fell considerably short of the seventeen-year Hall of Fame–worthy career of Buddy Myer.

Some of the longest careers of Jewish athletes have been in reserve roles. On the basis of a fifteen-year run as a backup catcher for five teams, Moe Berg was the quintessential unsung Jewish athlete, because the story of Moe Berg extends far beyond his catching. A Princeton graduate, Berg reportedly parachuted into Europe to gather undercover information for the United States during World War II. There is ordinarily no distinction for a catcher with a

.243 career batting average and a career total of 6 home runs over fifteen years. The National Baseball Hall of Fame houses Moe Berg's Presidential Medal of Freedom.

Berg was not the only Jewish journeyman catcher in baseball. Joe Ginsberg served primarily in the fifties as a backup catcher for seven teams. The following decade, Norm Sherry hung on as a defensive specialist catcher for five years with two teams. More recently, catcher Jesse Levis established himself as a contemporary version of the journeyman Ginsberg by playing on six teams over nearly ten years. Eric Helfand had a brief stay in the big leagues as a catcher after putting power numbers in college. In 2002, David Newhan attempted to catch on with the Los Angeles Dodgers after being cut by the Philadelphia Phillies.

There have been Jewish defensive specialists at many positions. On the weight of a slick glove, light-hitting Eddy

Al Schacht performed as "The Clown Prince of Baseball" for decades after his brief pitching career ended. (Photo courtesy of Al Schacht.)

Zodsky had a cup of coffee in the big leagues as a utility player. Norm Miller made a ten-year career by playing centerfield for the Astros and Braves.

During the spectacular run by Sandy Koufax in the sixties, the burden of great potential was put on Howie Kitt and Mickey Abarbanel by the New York Yankees and Chicago White Sox. Neither ever made the major leagues.

In 2002, Andrew Lorraine and Tony Cogan faced difficult odds at extending their brief careers. Keith Glauber had shown promise as a relief pitcher until an arthroscopically repaired right rotator cuff robbed him of his speed.

There have been several unsung Jewish hockey goalies. Over the course of four years in the seventies, goalie Bernie Wolfe attracted a small Jewish following, even wearing a mask, for an upstart Washington Capital franchise in a city that was new to hockey. Mike Veisor had a brief run as a goalie in the seventies. Veisor had wanted to become the first Jewish goalie in the National Hockey League, but Ross Brooks made it first. Two decades later, Todd Simon had a brief run in the National Hockey league as well.

Herman Barron finally scored a hole in one at fifty-four years old while competing as a senior after a successful career on the pro golf tour during the 1930s and 1940s. A young Marty Fleckman burst into sudden but short-lived prominence by winning the 1967 Cajun Classic in his first tournament as a professional golfer. In 1973, I asked Fleckman what part religion has played in his career. "Religion really has not played any part in my career as I can see, except for the special following by Jewish fans that cheer me on," he said.

In 1990, Tony Sills became the first Jewish golfer since Fleckman to gain significant attention with a win at the 1990 Independent Insurance Agent Open. He had previously won the 1971 Los Angeles City Junior Open, the 1976 Southern California Amateur, the 1981 Queen Mary Open, and 1981 Coors Open.

In football, Phil Handler made All-America Honorable Mention in 1929 at Texas Christian University and played six years for the Chicago Cardinals at offensive guard. He ultimately served as head coach of the team for one season.

Irv Mondschein was national Collegiate Athletic Association high jump champion in 1947 and 1948 and held both the indoor and outdoor Intercollegiate Athletic Association records. He was Amateur Athletic Union national champion in the decathlon in 1944, 1946, and 1947 and runner-up in 1948 and 1949.

As a coach at the University of Pennsylvania, Mondschein inspired future medical doctor Jeff Fried to win the 1973 Maccabiah Gold high jump medal. A year later, Fried told me, "There aren't many Jewish athletes; so as a Jewish athlete, I've always felt I was representative of a large number of Jews and not just myself."

Arthur Tauber completed his college fencing career undefeated. From 1940 through 1941, Tauber held the intercollegiate epee championship; and in 1942, he became intercollegiate foil champion.

Norman Sper Jr. was inducted into the International Swimming Hall of Fame after winning the National Diving Championship in 1944, 1945, and 1949.

USA Maccabiah rugby player Josh Henkin (right) received inspiration to excel as both an athlete and scholar from his grandmother, Selma Lavenstein Jacobs. (Photo courtesy of Josh Henkin.)

Sylvia Martin was named Woman Bowler of the Year in 1955 and 1960 after twice bowling perfect games of 300.

Eadie Wetzel earned induction into the International Swimming Hall of Fame in 1968 for setting a world record to win the National 200-meter Freestyle Championship.

Success at one endeavor seldom comes at the sacrifice of another. It does not take a Shawn Green to disprove the ridiculous notion that most Jewish people tend not to be good at sports. People who are successful in sports do not necessarily succeed as students, but most people who succeed in academic pursuits tend to be successful as athletes, too. Not despite but because of their disproportionate brilliance in the arts and sciences are so many Jewish people so very athletic. For each of the top hundred Jewish athletes of all time, there have always been thousands of successful Jewish athletes—such as my cousin Josh Henkin, who, in addition to being a Maccabiah gold and silver medalist in rugby, is a scholar.

Chapter 6

Jewish Sports
Team Executives

Barney Dreyfuss was the first nonplayer to make the National Baseball Hall of Fame. The World Series was his idea. Until Babe Ruth came to New York and made the Yankees a dynasty, the most successful franchise had been Dreyfuss's Pittsburgh Pirates—a team he built from scratch.

Gabe Paul built a reputation as a shrewd trader as general manager of the Cleveland Indians during the 1960s and of the New York Yankees during the following decade.

In 1973, I raised the question regarding why there aren't more Jews in sports. This was his reply: "I think if you will check statistics, you will find that the number of Jewish athletes on professional teams is very close to the overall percentage of the population of this country."

After the resignation of Stephen Greenberg as deputy commissioner of Major League Baseball, the next and current commissioner happened to be Jewish anyway; but, unlike Stephen Greenberg—who played minor league baseball—Bud Selig came to the position as an owner.

In professional football, some ten years before George Allen would coin the slogan "The future is now" as coach of the Washington Redskins, Allie Sherman realized similar success from relying on veterans who were thought by others to have been over-the-hill. From 1961 through 1963, Sherman coached the New York Giants to National Football League Eastern Division titles and was twice named Coach of the Year.

In thirty-one years under Barney Dreyfuss, the Pittsburgh Pirates won two World Series and six National League pennants. (Photo courtesy of the Pittsburgh Pirates.)

Sid Gillman introduced game films and the two-platoon system to professional football; but before that, he played in the first College All-Star Football Game as an All-America Honorable Mention. In 1955, Gillman coached the Los Angeles Rams to a Western Division title in his first year as their head coach. When the American Football League was founded five years later, he moved on to the new league as a head coach and general manager of the San Diego Chargers. In 1963, his Chargers anchored a passing offense behind Ron Mix and won the American Football

League Championship. He is best remembered for using films to study opponents, formalizing the two-platoon system, and putting names on players' jerseys.

Future team owner Carroll Rosenbloom played halfback for the University of Pennsylvania's football team and pitched for Penn's baseball team. Rosenbloom traded the entire Baltimore Colts franchise he owned for the Los Angeles Rams. In 1973, I asked him to comment on the public relations service that Jewish athletes provide to American Jewry. This was his response: "Most Jewish athletes perform a valuable public relations service for American Jews. Certainly, Sandy Koufax did because of his great talent, intelligence, modesty, courage, and exemplary behavior."

Sonny Werblin headed a five-man syndicate that purchased a then-bankrupt New York American Football League franchise and outbid the established National Football League for some of the top collegiate players. That forced a merger between the two leagues. His New York Jets won the third Super Bowl in 1969 over the heavily favored Baltimore Colts. I posed several questions to Werblin for my *Jewish Athletes' Hall of Fame* in 1973, and this was his response: "I have no comment for your book, since as an American, I think there is too much polarization in this country as it is." What Sonny Werblin said is true; but the opposite of polarization is assimilation, and its extraordinary consequence has been a dwindling Jewish population.

Oakland Raider managing general partner Al Davis made the Pro Football Hall of Fame after having been the driving force during the sixties for a merger between the old American and National Football Leagues. He is chief executive of the franchise that is a perennial Super Bowl contender and champion.

Norman Bramam owned the Philadelphia Eagles from 1985 through 1994. According to a 1985 *USA Today* article, Bramam was an activist in support of Jewish causes.

In 1973, some twenty-seven years before his Baltimore Ravens would become Super Bowl champions, owner Art Modell replied to my question on the lack of Jews in sports in this way:

I guess that the reason there are not so many professional Jewish athletes stems from the fact that our parents from the time we were very young tried to direct us in the careers of law, medicine, and other similar professions. Seriously, you must remember that the Jewish population constitutes a very small part of this country.

A little-known story about Modell shows him to be a man of extraordinary compassion. With Jimmy Brown in his backfield, Modell had the greatest fullback ever to play the game before trading for the draft rights of Heisman Trophy–winning halfback Ernie Davis in 1962. But Davis was diagnosed with a terminal case of leukemia and died without ever joining Brown in the backfield. Modell could have attempted to void the trade and retain the future Hall of Fame player in Bobby Mitchell, whom he had traded to acquire Davis. Instead, he protected Davis from the tragic news of his own pending demise. As beat reporter for the *Plain Dealer* in Cleveland, Chuck Heaton covered the Ernie Davis affair from its mysterious start to its sad finish. He shared with me this inside story:

> Modell . . . called the late Frank Gibbons, who was covering the All Star game for The Press, and me, and asked us not to publicize the nature of the illness because Davis had not been informed. . . . The Browns finally announced that he had leukemia some months later, after there was a remission and Ernie was feeling better.

Another compassionate member of the professional football establishment is former coach Marv Levy, a recent inductee into the Pro Football Hall of Fame. He coached his Buffalo Bills to an unprecedented four consecutive Super Bowls. However, it was a comment published in *USA Today* before his first Super Bowl appearance that revealed the extraordinary nature of his sensitivity. The subject was hunting, and Levy made it clear that it was not for him: "One minute a bird is alive enjoying his day and the next minute he's dead—no, thank you."

Jerry Wolman focused on the business aspects of his Philadelphia Eagles when he owned them in the 1960s, but Dan Snyder is taking an opposite approach as owner of the Washington Redskins now. Snyder makes many of the team's player transactions and is directly involved in the recruitment of free agents

Co-owner and general manager of championship teams in both professional basketball and football, Max Winter had been a

Marv Levy was the first coach to reach four consecutive Super Bowls and along with Art Modell, among the most compassionate too. (Photo by Robert L. Smith, courtesy of the Buffalo Bills.)

noted gymnast and ice skater in Austria. His National Basketball Association Minneapolis Lakers won five divisional and two world championships over a five-year span; in addition, his National Football League Minnesota Vikings made return trips to the Super Bowl.

In 1977, the Washington Bullets basketball franchise that Abe Pollin owned won the National Basketball Association World Championship. He celebrated by taking the team to Israel—only to lose to the Israeli National Team in an extraordinary upset. Pollin later renamed the team the Wizards. He also founded the Washington Capitols National Hockey League team.

In 1973, I interviewed Pollin in his office. "When injustice affects only Jews, the burden of informing the rest of the world rests upon the Jewish voice," he said. I also asked him if he thought there was a stereotype of a weakling Jew. "If there ever was a stereotype of a weakling Jew, Israel has certainly demolished that; and Jewish athletes reinforce the message," he replied.

Harry Glickman's relatives died at Treblinka. He spoke out publicly whenever a politician minimized the Holocaust. Glickman built a potential dynasty with the Portland Trailblazers, which won a National Basketball Association championship in 1977 with unselfish team play, only to see it crumble with foot injuries to center Bill Walton.

Red Auerbach coached the Boston Celtics to eight consecutive National Basketball Association Championships—a feat that may never again be equaled in any sport. His patented victory cigar was an anticipated climax to every game he coached. In 1973, I asked him about his perceptions of Jews in sports. "Jewish athletes perform a great public relations service for American Jews," he replied. "I feel that most of the American Jews take pride in the Jewish athletes and their accomplishments, because I hear

Red Auerbach built his Celtic dynasty with a strategy that relied on defense and passing, rather than great individual heroics. He was inducted into the Professional Basketball Hall of Fame. (Photo courtesy of the Boston Celtics.)

these comments wherever I go. As a matter of fact, they always want to know why there aren't more of them, but that in itself is another problem."

Larry Brown gained admittance to the Naismith Memorial Basketball Hall of Fame as a coach in 2002. His Indiana Pacers and Philadelphia 76er teams reached the National Basketball Association playoff finals. His greatest coaching achievement may have been taking a Los Angeles Clipper team of castoffs to a rare playoff berth. As a college coach, Brown led his University of Kansas squad to the National Collegiate Athletic Association championship in 1988 after having reached the Final Four with the same squad two years earlier. His 1981 UCLA Bruins team was a semifinalist. He played on the 1964 Gold Medal winning United States team in the Tokyo Olympics and, as a professional, in the American Basketball League. Brown helped coach the 1968 and 1974 United States teams.

Basketball coach Larry Brown was one of the few coaches to change teams often and continually succeed with entirely different styles of play. (Photo courtesy of the San Antonio Spurs.)

Red Holzman coached the New York Knicks teams that won National Basketball Association championships in 1970 and 1973. Among those he coached in earning his way into the National Basketball Hall of Fame was future senator Bill Bradley.

As assistant coach, Ron Rothstein was the defensive genius behind the Detroit Pistons' repeat National Basketball Association Championship teams that came to be known as "The Bad Boys." He went on to become the first head coach of the Miami Heat and later returned to Detroit as head coach of the by-then over-the-hill Pistons. Rothstein was too early with the Heat and too late with the Pistons—which is the story of many people's lives.

Nat Fleischer's all-time rankings became an institution in professional boxing to the extent that the honor was so universally known that it was regarded to be prestigious as a championship belt.

The entire starting five of the New York Knicks team that Red Holzman coached made the Hall of Fame. (Photo courtesy of the New York Knicks.)

Chapter 7

The Jewish
Sports Following

In my 1989 book, *The Jewish Athletes' Hall of Fame*, I introduced the
All-Time Ranking of Great Jewish Athletes, which compares athletes from different sports against one another, but it entirely
missed major stars whose religion had escaped other authors on
the subject as well.

Release of that book provided me with the most extraordinary
resource of information about Jewish athletes imaginable. It
brought letters from all over the world advising me of Jewish
athletes I had missed. On tour, I also met a great many Jewish
people who not only followed great Jews in sports but had participated as well.

Accomplishments of great Jewish athletes do not come as a
surprise to many Jews. I have discovered that in appearances at
Jewish Community Centers in Rochester, Rockville, the District
of Columbia, Norfolk, Fort Lauderdale, and Miami. That is prob-
ably because so many Jewish people tend to be physically fit, if
not gifted in sports.

However, the notion that there have been many Jewish athletes
did surprise one man. He turned to me in near hysterics after just
glancing at the cover of my first book, *The Jewish Athletes' Hall of
Fame* on a train leaving New York. I had appeared there at the
Jewish Heritage Book Festival on a panel with Ira Berkow,
columnist for *The New York Times*; Vic Segal, then sports editor of
the *Daily News*; and Steve Wulf, then a senior editor of *Sports Illustrated*, who served as moderator. There were more Jewish athletes than we had time to discuss before the audience, yet the

cover of my book rendered the man on the train into seemingly uncontrollable laughter. Finally, he managed to ask, "Do you mean there's more than one?"

I was guest on a radio station WNBH, out of New Bedford, Massachusetts, and fielded questions about Jewish athletes from Jack Peterson, Russ Baldwin, and Bernie Picinisko just before the release of my next book, *Defending Animals' Rights Is the Right Thing to Do*. In an apparent Howard Cosell imitation, Peterson suggested that I follow those two books with one entitled "The Jewish Dog's Hall of Fame."

Despite the funny jokes, however, great Jewish athletes have compared favorably to the greatest of athletes in all of sports. Statistics do not tell the entire story. In almost every sport, changes in conditions favor current athletes.

These changes range from a livelier ball and alleged use of steroids in baseball to tolerance of traveling restrictions and the addition of a 3-point shot in basketball. The one constant intangible is the relative standing an athlete held in a particular sport. Certain comparisons are tempting: Dolph Schayes with Larry Bird, Benny Leonard with Roberto Duran, Ken Holtzman with Tom Glavine, Dick Savitt with Pete Sampras, Benny Friedman with Dan Marino, Barney Ross with Sugar Ray Leonard, Nat Holman with Jason Kidd, Battling Levinsky with Tommy "Hit Man" Hearns, Al Rosen with Cal Ripkin, Ted "Kid" Lewis with Felix Trinidad, Buddy Myer with Nellie Fox, Maxie Rosenbloom with Muhammad Ali on the downside of his career or Jimmy Young at his prime, Abe Attell with Salvador Sanchez, Harry Newman with Steve Young, Nancy Lieberman with Chamique Holdshaw, Louis "Kid" Kaplan with Julio Cesar Chavez, Jackie Fields with Ray "Boom-Boom" Mancini, Rudy LaRusso with Reggie Miller, Harry Danning with Elston Howard, and the capability of Sid Gordon to put up respectable power numbers while seldom striking out with that of Don Mattingly. However, most of the Jews who formed the basis of those comparisons have long since retired.

The dwindling Jewish presence in sports is an obvious reflection of a decline in the general population of Jews—a decline brought about first by the Holocaust and then through assimilation. The increasing scarcity of Jews compounds the problem by making it increasingly more convenient for Jewish people to select Gentiles, if they ever marry or have children at all. At the Jewish Community Center in Norfolk, a woman implied that she knew the reason for a decline of Jewish athletes. She asked how many of the athletes I praised had married Jewish women, how many of them were raising children to be Jewish.

A concern over a gradual decline in Jewish athletes was expressed in letters from two certified public accountants, Richard Brouse of California and Neil Keller of Maryland. "I wonder if all the exceptional people who are Jewish will be out of the gene pool by virtue of their non-Jewish children," Brouse wrote. Keller's letter pointed out that the representation of Jewish athletes used to include a superstar in almost every major sport. It no longer did.

I received a letter with similar sentiments from Shelly Sidlow of California. "As a child growing up in Chicago," he wrote, "we all had sports idols. Of course, they had to be Jewish . . . Benny Friedman, Marshall Goldberg, Sid Luckman, of my Chicago Bears team, Rosen and Danning in baseball, Ross in boxing. . . . Today, times are changing."

A letter from Rabbi Norman Kahan indicated that he had participated in college in baseball, basketball, boxing, and wrestling. Rabbi Kahan served then as the family rabbi of New York Mets president Fred Wilpon. He revealed that Wilpon played on the same high school baseball team as Sandy Koufax and that Wilpon's son Jeff was signed as a catcher with the Montreal Expos.

I was referred to bowlers Mark Roth and Marshall Holman in a letter from Gerald F. Simon of Beverly Hills. He also shared this story: "I had the pleasure of having Mike Epstein working for me in my construction company the summer before he started in college. . . . He came to my home the day he received his signing bonus from the Baltimore Orioles to show me his check."

Nathaniel H. Goldman, of Ohio, wrote that boxing champion Barney Ross had grown up on the Lower East Side of Manhattan with his father. "I can't tell you how much pride I felt, when I visited the Baseball Hall of Fame in Cooperstown in 1984 and took pictures of the plaques honoring Sandy Koufax and Hank Greenberg," he wrote.

From South Africa, Sam Woolf referred me to Jewish athletes of his country in tennis players Abe Segal, Syd Levy, and Julie

Mayer; rugby player Okey (Aaron) Geffin; track stars Harold Bromberg and the Sandler brothers; and cricket player Ali Bacher.

I talked with a woman at my appearance in Norfolk who had played basketball with Nancy Lieberman and a man, who was a former Maccabiah medalist, in Rochester.

At the District of Columbia Center, filmmaker Jeff Krulik advised me of such Jewish National Football League players as Harris Barton, Brad Edelman, and Alan Veingrad. Producer Aviva Kempner told me that she was producing a documentary film on Hank Greenberg because "he was a beacon of hope to millions of American Jews who faced bigotry during the Depression and World War II years." Ironically, in my subsequent appearance at the Jewish Community Center of Miami, I met a gentleman who had recently attended the Jewish wedding of Alan Veingrad—but by then, Veingrad's brief career had ended.

This photograph of body building champion David Leibowitz was given to me during my book tour for The Jewish Athletes' Hall of Fame *at the Jewish Community Center in Miami, by his grandmother Harriet Falk, a proud and elegant Jewish woman who encouraged his athleticism. (Photo courtesy of Harriet Falk.)*

At the Jewish Community Center in Miami, I was given a photograph of body builder David Leibowitz—grandson of Harriet Falk and son of Helene Falk Leibowitz, the center's senior adults director; in the audience was a former college soccer player who had rejected overtures to be a place kicker from the National Football League.

At the Jewish Community Center in Norfolk, book fair coordinator Rebecca Tabakin introduced me to the brother of Jewish baseball scout Harry Postave—who discovered baseball Hall of Famer Louis Aparicio—and to a rabbi who knew that former baseball pitcher Mark Clear was Jewish.

Disproportionate brilliance in the arts and sciences can somehow create a fallaciously debilitated stereotype of a Jewish person as a weakling whose only defense is an arsenal of trite clichés. That is why Jewish athletes are an irresistible attraction for so many Jews. They bask in reflected glory. The extraordinary consequence of accepting Cosell's depiction of sports as a microcosm of society is to look at famous Jewish athletes another way and see the people whose dreams they fulfill.

By transferring their acclaim to American Jewry, great Jewish athletes end the stereotype for the time being. But that does not end the anti-Semitism that inevitably results from preposterous

With his halting New York accent, he was the most exciting sportscaster ever. Howard Cosell electrified boxing and football fans with calls that became more memorable than the events. His repetitive scream—"Down goes Frazier!"— became part of nonsports jargon; but this was his most famous call: "Wait a minute. Wait a minute! Liston is not coming out. He's out! The winner and new heavyweight champion is Cassius Clay." If sportscaster Howard Cosell was right when he depicted sports as a microcosm of society, the fading presence of great Jewish athletes reflects a dwindling Jewish population. (Photo courtesy of ABC Sports.)

statements by a never-ending line of "irresponsible" public figures. Throughout history, they have singled Jews out as the
scapegoat for economic downturns and international events with
the same lie—that a small minority of predominately assimilated
Jewish people somehow holds an impossible majority control of
the media, banks, and Congress. It makes no sense at all.

But from Charles Lindbergh and Joseph Kennedy to Billy Gra-
ham and Richard Nixon; George Brown and Jesse Jackson to
Louis Farrakhan and Pat Buchanan; and David Duke to Jim
Moran, only the names who say such things change.

Not long after receiving a publishing contract for my first
book, I received a call from the public relations director of a National Football League team. He asked me whether my book was
"pro or con." It seemed funny then that someone could even con-
jure the notion of a book that would be critical of Jews in sports;
but those individuals—the Pat Buchanans of the world—they
would find a way.

The public tends to judge a whole people's caliber by their
most physically gifted individuals, and what they say is often inferred to be representative of the people who make up their following. I asked the most famous Jewish athletes of this century
what responsibility they perceive that their extraordinary Jewish
followings put on them.

The famous Jewish athletes varied in their responses regarding
whether prominent Jews in sports have an obligation to use their
prominence in support of interests that are of unique concern to
Jewish people—in other words, responding to a public figure's
anti-Semitic remark.

Andy Cohen was unequivocal in his opinion that they do. The
old baseball New York Giants needed a second baseman to replace traded Hall of Famer Rogers Hornsby. "I considered myself
a representative of Jewish fans," he said.

Lou Gordon emerged as a consensus All-American tackle at
the University of Illinois. "I considered myself an individual
player and felt no obligation to stand up and act as a representative for the fans in matters of social interest," Gordon said.

Hall of Fame football quarterback Sid Luckman introduced the
T-formation. "My talents were strictly athletic, and whenever
called upon to speak publicly, it was always in relation to my
sport and the people connected with it. As athletes, I don't think

we are qualified or well enough informed to voice opinions on grave issues," he said.

Basketball Hall of Fame legend Dolph Schayes established himself as one of the greatest big men of his day. "Public opinion is influenced by attention getters—whether they be athletes or politicians—speaking intelligently on any issue," he said.

While in the minor leagues, Stephen Greenberg wrote this in a letter to me:

It is important for people in the spotlight to be extremely careful when making public statements because of the impact they have on millions of people. But whenever an athlete—or anyone else—feels strongly about a political or social condition in the world, it should be his prerogative to speak out and try to call attention to iniquities he perceives.

In the 1950s, Al Rosen became the first Major League Baseball player to unanimously win the Most Valuable Player award. He had this to say in response to my question: "It is incumbent upon Jews everywhere to become well-known spokesmen for the Jewish religion. I feel that Jewish athletes, particularly because of the publicity given to their acts, should always be aware of their heritage and act accordingly."

Hall of Fame baseball pitcher Sandy Koufax stunned the Gentile world in 1965 by sitting out the first game of the World Series in observance of the Jewish Day of Atonement, Yom Kippur. "My personal feelings have always remained private, and I would prefer to keep it that way," he said.

Ron Mix earned Pro Football Hall of Fame induction as an offensive lineman. "All people have a responsibility to call attention to injustices that exist anywhere within world society. That one is a personal; victim, of course, makes the interest in doing so more personal; but the fervor should be the same. We truly do live within a world community wherein isolated events affect all eventually. Thus, there is a selfish reason to correct injustices even if one is motivated altruistically."

Former Israeli Olympic soccer team captain Roby Young gained an enormous Jewish following while playing the New York Cosmos. "Yes, I do think that Jewish athletes should use their prominence to exert influence on public opinion," he said.

Janet Haas won a silver medal in tennis at the Ninth Maccabiah Games. She said, "Jewish athletes should discuss Jewish issues with their rabbis or other knowledgeable Jews and then use their prominence to exert influence on public opinion. Like many black athletes, Jewish athletes can influence other Jews to act on matters."

Brian Gottfried, then a leading professional tennis star, disagreed. "Sports and politics should be kept separate. The two have very little in common, and it takes a different type of person to do each," he said.

Jeff Fried, a 1973 Maccabiah gold medalist in track, agreed. "As a Jewish athlete, I always felt I was responsible of a large number of Jews and not just myself," he said.

Heavyweight boxer Peter Brodsky reached the final round of the New Jersey Golden Gloves Boxing Championship in 1972. "If Jewish athletes would join together . . . maybe we could enlighten some people about the various tragedies that have befallen Jewish people," he said.

Nancy Ornstein won the Middle Atlantic Women's tennis Championship two years after the tragic 1972 Olympics. "The Jewish athlete lucky enough to have influence should use it to our advantage," she said.

Basketball and also then hockey team owner Abe Pollin said, "I think it is incumbent on every Jew to recognize when an injustice against humanity has taken place and to enlighten others about that injustice. . . . When that injustice affects only Jews," he added, "the burden of informing the rest of the world rests upon the Jewish voice."

The late Carroll Rosenbloom built championship football teams on both coasts. "Most Jewish athletes perform a valuable public relations service for American Jews. Certainly, Sandy Koufax because of his great talent, intelligence, modesty, courage, and exemplary behavior."

Before becoming owner of the Philadelphia Eagles, Norman Bramam was reported in the *USA Today* to have protested with Jewish activists on behalf of Jews elsewhere.

The late newspaper columnist Morrie Siegel said, "I would like to see Jewish athletes speak out on Jewish issues the way black athletes do on black issues."

In his book *I Never Played the Game* (Morrow, 1985), Howard Cosell recalled the highly publicized uproar by the National Association for the Advancement of Colored People that followed selection by the American Broadcasting Company of a Super Bowl announcing tandem that did not include O. J. Simpson. Perhaps there would have been pressure put on the Yankees to fire Billy Martin for not pitching Ken Holtzman if Jews had caused a similar uproar, but no Jewish group or Jewish celebrity said anything at all.

Famous Jewish athletes could lend a strong voice of defense whenever a public figure attempts to project Jews as scapegoats. They could express outrage whenever a public figure tries to intimidate Jews from expressing opinions out of fear that it would lend credence to the lies perpetuated about so-called Jewish control.

The contention that a small minority of predominately assimilated Jewish people somehow holds an impossible majority control of the media, banks, and Congress is so obviously wrong; it reflects stupidity . Unfortunately, it is too ignorant a remark for most prominent Jewish people to even dignify with a response. And its obvious lack of logic not only gives the false appearance of being harmless but projects a simple-minded innocence in the public figure.

The simple-minded innocence projected to those who say it is analogous to the almost endearing way that many late-night television comedians portrayed the vicious attack on 1994 skating silver medalist Nancy Kerrigan. The attack was conspired to deprive her of an opportunity to compete for the benefit of her oblivious opponent, Tonya Harding.

But never had as high a profile crime been so terribly bungled. In his July 14–28, 1994, *Rolling Stone* article, Randall Sullivan quoted Harding's former husband, Jeff Gillooly, in sarcastically asking a coconspirator whether a certain word reflecting extremely low intelligence appeared on a certain part of him; and because of how foolish the crime was to commit, the question later evolved into a popular mode of self-deprecating humor. Of course, Gillooly knew what he was doing. There is no simple-minded innocence in public figures who contend that Jews have too much power, either. They know the vulnerability to attacks from others that Jewish people face as a result of their statements and the intimidation of Jews they create when saying it.

The lie is very damaging, and it is never innocently said. It has long been known to result in anti-Semitic attacks on Jewish people every time a public figure says it.

History has shown that every lie about Jewish people requires a response. A famous Jewish athlete, even a former one, can respond to anti-Semitic remarks by other public figures in ways that a Jewish following cannot.

Chapter 8

Milestones in Jewish Sports History

- February 1, 1904. Abe Attell knocked out Harry Forbes in the fifth round to win the World Featherweight Championship.
- January 1, 1911. In New York City, Henry Benjamin Greenberg—the greatest Jewish athlete and arguably the greatest right-handed hitter in baseball history—was born.
- August 31, 1915. Ted "Kid" Lewis scored a fifteen-round decision over Jack Britton to win the World Welterweight Championship.
- October 9, 1915. With a young Babe Ruth sitting on the Red Sox bench awaiting his next run to pitch, Philadelphia Phillie Erskine Mayer lost the second game of the Baseball World Series in the bottom of the ninth inning in a 2–1 pitchers' duel.
- May 28, 1917. Benny Leonard knocked out Freddie Welsh in the ninth round to win the World Lightweight Championship.
- November 6, 1918. World light heavyweight champion Battling Levinsky nearly scored what would have been among the greatest upset victories in sports' history by knocking down legendary heavyweight champion Jack Dempsey twice in the second round of a losing effort.
- February 12, 1922. Nat Holman achieved what may have been the first recorded basketball "triple double" by scoring

more than 10 points, hauling down more than 10 rebounds, and making more than 10 assists in a single game.

- July 24, 1923. World lightweight champion Benny Leonard retained his title on a fifteen-round decision over Lew Tendler.
- January 2, 1925. Louis "Kid" Kaplan knocked out Danny Kramer in the ninth round to win the World Featherweight Championship.
- January 10, 1928. Baseball's New York Giants handed the second base job to Andy Cohen by trading legendary second baseman Rogers Hornsby to the Boston Red Sox.
- December 13, 1929. Green Bay ended a near perfect year for the New York Giants football team, which had outscored its opponents behind quarterback Benny Friedman by more than 4 points to 1 until its defeat by the Packers in a bad weather game.
- June 25, 1930. Maxie Rosenbloom slapped his way past Jimmy Slattery in a fifteen-round defensive battle to become the New York light heavyweight champion.
- January 28, 1932. Jackie Fields won the World Welterweight Championship for the second time on a ten-round decision over Lou Brouillard.
- December 16, 1933. Harry Newman completed 13 consecutive passes without an incompletion or interception in leading the New York Giants over the Chicago Bears in the National Football League Championship Game.
- June 8, 1933. A year before he would win the World Heavyweight Championship, Max Baer knocked out Nazi Germany's sports idol Max Schmeling in the tenth round of a brutal fight with a Jewish Star of David on his trunks.
- September 12, 1933. Barney Ross won a fifteen-round decision over Tony Canzoneri to win the World Lightweight and Junior Welterweight Championships.
- October 5, 1933. Buddy Myer's 3 hits sparked the Washington Nationals over the New York Giants in game three of the Baseball World Series.
- April 15, 1935. Obviously not expecting to fill the void left by their sale of Babe Ruth fifteen years earlier, the Boston Red Sox signed multilingual and light-hitting backup catcher Moe

Berg as a free agent; but Berg ironically outhit a by then over-the-hill Ruth by more than 100 points that year.

- October 9, 1937. New York Giant catcher Harry Danning's 3 hits overtook the champion New York Yankees in game four of the baseball World Series.
- January 1, 1937. Running back Marshall Goldberg carried the University of Pittsburgh over the University of Washington as the first Jewish football player to play in the Rose Bowl.
- October 2, 1938. Hank Greenberg's incredible run at Babe Ruth's single-season home run record—which had seen him climb to within two at fifty-eight with five games left to play—ended on the last game of the season as opposing pitchers continued their apparent conspiracy to keep the ball out of the strike zone and thereby deprive him of any chance at the record.
- November 14, 1943. Quarterback Sid Luckman threw 7 touchdown passes to carry the Chicago Bears to victory over the football New York Giants.
- December 14, 1949. Leo Durocher traded away Sid Gordon at his prime almost twenty-one years before he would foolishly rid another team of his of a spectacular young and already a double no-hit pitcher, Ken Holtzman.
- February 27, 1950. Max Zaslofsky scored 35 points to lead his Chicago Bulls over the Boston Celtics.
- July 11, 1951. In defeating Ken McGregor, Dick Savitt became the first Jewish player to win the Wimbledon Lawn Tennis Championship only to be inexplicably left off the United States Davis Cup Team.
- January 17, 1952. Dolph Schayes lifted his Syracuse Nationals basketball team over the Minneapolis Lakers with 41 points.
- July 11, 1954. In the friendly confines of Cleveland Stadium, third baseman Al Rosen slugged 2 home runs to win the 1954 All-Star Game for the American League.
- April 8, 1957. Lenny Rosenbluth carried the University of North Carolina over Wilt Chamberlain's heavily favored University of Kansas team to win the National Collegiate Athletic Association Tournament.

- October 8, 1959. In saving the sixth and final game, World Series Most Valuable Player Larry Sherry surpassed the conventional expectations in baseball of a relief pitcher by stroking 2 hits himself.
- May 5, 1962. Los Angeles rookie Bo Belinsky pitched a no-hitter against the Baltimore Orioles.
- May 23, 1960. Hours after the announcement that Simon Wiesenthal had captured Nazi Adolf Eichmann, Sandy Koufax pitched a 1-hit shutout; and after entering the game with a career record of 28 games won and 31 lost—from that point on—compiled a staggering record of 111 games won against only 43 losses.
- March 27, 1963. National Collegiate Athletic Association Player of the Year Art Heyman scored 40 points and brought down 24 rebounds to carry Duke University to victory over the University of North Carolina.
- September 10, 1965. Sandy Koufax pitched his fourth no-hitter and only perfect game over the Chicago Cubs.
- August 4, 1966. Art Shamsky hit his 4th home run in as many at bats as a pinch hitter after slugging 3 in a single game two days earlier.
- June 3, 1971. Ken Holtzman shut down the Cincinnati Reds' "Big Red Machine" with his second no-hitter.
- September 7, 1972. Major League Baseball players Ken Holtzman, Mike Epstein, and Richie Scheinblum played with black armbands over their uniforms to protest the murders of eleven Jewish participants of the Munich Olympics where Mark Spitz had set a record for swimming by winning seven gold medals.
- August 26, 1978. Mike Rossman won the World Boxing Association Light Heavyweight Championship on a technical knockout over Victor Galindez.
- August 7, 1979. Ron Mix was inducted into the Pro Football Hall of Fame.
- July 9, 1980. On his way to winning the Cy Young Award, Steve Stone hurled three perfect innings in an ultimately losing effort for the American League All-Star team.
- January 29, 1995. Harris Barton's blocking bought extra time for quarterback Steve Young, enabling Young to engineer a blowout Super Bowl football victory.

- June 18, 1995. Corey Pavin won the United States Open Golf Tournament.
- July 13, 1999. Playing in his first baseball All-Star Game, Shawn Green chopped an infield single in his only at bat.
- September 3, 2001. Jay Fiedler made his debut as starting quarterback for the Dolphins by leading Miami to a 23–0 win over Seattle with 1 touchdown pass and no interceptions.
- September 26, 2001. Shawn Green observed Yom Kippur by not playing for the Los Angeles Dodgers in a pennant stretch game against the San Francisco Giants.
- May 23, 2002. Shawn Green stunned the baseball world by slugging a record-tying 4 homers, a double, and single in a single game.
- June 22, 2002. Shawn Green continued his torrid onslaught by smashing his 22nd homer in thirty-four games.

Chapter 9

The Jewish Sports History IQ Test

For items 1–10, please identify the Jewish athlete described.

1. This left-handed pitcher dated three movie stars and married a Playmate of the Year.
   — a. Ty Cobb   — c. Bo Belinsky
   — b. Haystacks Calhoun   — d. Buddy "Nature Boy" Rogers

2. This southpaw threw no-hitters against teams featuring Hank Aaron, Orlando Cepeda, Johnny Bench, and Tony Perez.
   — a. Whitey Ford   — c. Ken Holtzman
   — b. Sandy Koufax   — d. Steve Carlton

3. This slugger signed a six-year $84 million contract.
   — a. Hank Greenberg   — c. Shawn Green
   — b. Tiger Woods   — d. Ray "Boom-Boom" Mancini

4. This second baseman replaced Rogers Hornsby.
   — a. Eddy Zodsky   — c. Andy Cohen
   — b. Jackie Robinson   — d. Chuck Knoblauch

5. This woman won a silver medal in swimming.
   — a. Nancy Lieberman   — c. Marilyn Ramenofsky
   — b. Mia Hamm   — d. Amy Alcott

6. This swimmer won nine gold medals.
   — a. Peyton Manning   — c. Mark Spitz
   — b. Lou Gordon   — d. Sid Gordon

7. This son of a Hall of Famer became deputy commissioner of Major League Baseball after starring at Yale University in baseball and soccer.

—— a. George W. Bush   —— c. Stephen Greenberg
—— b. Sonny Hertzberg   —— d. Albert Gore Jr.

8. This boxer knocked out the idol of Nazi Germany, Max Schmeling.

—— a. Mike Tyson   —— c. Max Baer
—— b. Woody Allen   —— d. Shlomo Glickstein

9. This first baseman was Major League Baseball's first designated hitter.

—— a. Edgar Martinez   —— c. Ron Blomberg
—— b. Willie McCovey   —— d. George Stone

10. This player had the nickname "Super Jew" before he reached the Major Leagues.

—— a. Michael Jordan   —— c. Mike Epstein
—— b. Steve Stone   —— d. Pat Buchanan

For each set of analogies, mark the item representing the pair of athletes that best represents their relationships in terms of the standing that each of them held.

11. Sid Luckman : John Elway =

—— a. Kevin Grevey : Kobe Bryant
—— b. Kevin McHale : Juan Howard
—— c. Mickey Mantle : Barry Bonds
—— d. Rick Monday : Sammy Sosa

12. Dolph Schayes : Larry Bird =

—— a. Wally Bunker : Greg Maddox
—— b. Sonny Jurgenson : Trent Dilfer
—— c. Johnny Bench : Ivan Rodriguez
—— d. Chris Hanburger : Lawrence Taylor

13. Al Rosen : Cal Ripkin =

—— a. Kareem Abdul Jabbar : Ralph Sampson
—— b. Gayle Sayers : Joe Don Looney

—— c. Larry Brown : Walter Payton
—— d. Jeff Ruland : Shaquille O'Neal

14. Benny Friedman : Dan Marino =
—— a. Sammy Sosa : Mark McGwire
—— b. Roger Maris : Reggie Jackson
—— c. Pete Maravich : Anthony Peeler
—— d. John "Hot Plate" Williams : Shawn Kemp

15. Hank Greenberg : Lou Gehrig =
—— a. Drew Bledsoe : Rick Mirer
—— b. Bobby Dandridge : Julius Erving
—— c. Wilt Chamberlain : Bill Russell
—— d. Don Bosseler : Jim Brown

For the last five questions, mark next to the item that identifies the Gentile athletes.

16. —— a. Dick Savitt   —— c. Bjorn Borg
    —— b. Lyle Alzado   —— d. Harry Newman

17. —— a. Jackie Fields   —— c. Joe Theisman
    —— b. Harris Barton   —— d. Brad Gilbert

18. —— a. Larry Sherry   —— c. Billy Martin
    —— b. Elliott Maddox   —— d. Ross Brooks

19. —— a. Dolph Schayes   —— c. Leo Durocher
    —— b. Ron Mix   —— d. Ted "Kid" Lewis

20. —— a. Benny Leonard   —— c. Sugar Ray Leonard
    —— b. Barry Asher   —— d. Rudy LaRusso

THE KEY TO THE JEWISH SPORTS HISTORY IQ TEST

Scoring the test is simple: Every correct answer is c.

1. This left-handed pitcher dated three movie stars and married a Playmate of the Year.

   c. Bo Belinsky.

   On *The Dating Game*, Bo would have won. Ty Cobb was crude and unsociable, Haystacks Calhoun weighed more than six hundred pounds, and the "Nature Boy" strutted.

2. This southpaw threw no-hitters against teams featuring Hank Aaron, Orlando Cepeda, Johnny Bench, and Tony Perez.

c. Ken Holtzman.

Koufax threw no-hitters against the Mets, Giants, Phillies, and Cubs. Whitey Ford never threw a no-hitter and was not Jewish; neither was Steve Carlton. The April 14, 1994, editions of the *Washington Post* and *USA Today* reported the American Jewish Congress rescinding its request of the National Baseball Hall of Fame to bar Carlton's induction that year until he apologized for remarks published in a magazine (that had quoted Carlton as allegedly saying that "twelve Jewish bankers ruled the world" and were "plotting against 'us'") after Carlton denied that he had said them.

3. This slugger signed a six-year $84 million contract.

c. Shawn Green.

Hank Greenberg was the highest paid player of his game, but salaries had not reached that level when he played.

4. This second baseman replaced Rogers Hornsby.

c. Andy Cohen.

Andy Cohen faced much of the discrimination that Jackie Robinson endured.

5. This woman won a silver medal in swimming.

c. Marilyn Ramenofsky.

Ramenofsky is the only swimmer, and Hamm is not Jewish.

6. This swimmer won nine gold medals.

c. Mark Spitz.

Peyton Manning is not Jewish and the two Gordons played football and baseball, respectively. The seven gold medals that Mark Spitz won is the greatest achievement in the history of competitive swimming.

7. This son of a National Baseball Hall of Famer became deputy commissioner of Major League Baseball after starring at Yale University in baseball and soccer.

   c. Stephen Greenberg.

   President Bush and Vice President Gore both had famous fathers, but neither made the Hall of Fame.

8. This boxer knocked out the idol of Nazi Germany, Max Schmeling.

   c. Max Baer.

   Baer had only a strain of Jewish heritage, and Tyson has no Jewish heritage at all; but if Tyson had been alive then, he would have annihilated Schmeling, too.

9. This first baseman was Major League Baseball's first designated hitter.

   c. Ron Blomberg.

   Ron Blomberg was the first designated hitter, but Edgar Martinez is still the greatest.

10. This player had the nickname "Super Jew" before he reached the Major Leagues.

    c. Mike Epstein.

    For each set of analogies, mark the item representing the pair of athletes that best represents their relationships in terms of their standing that each of them held.

11. Sid Luckman : John Elway =

    c. Mickey Mantle : Barry Bonds.

    Sid Luckman and John Elway were two of the greatest quarterbacks in football history. That level of greatness was achieved by both athletes in only one of the groupings, Mickey Mantle and Barry Bonds.

12. Dolph Schayes : Larry Bird =

    c. Johnny Bench : Ivan Rodriguez.

    Dolph Schayes and Larry Bird were two of the greatest forwards ever to grace a basketball court; that level of comparable greatness was achieved by both athletes in only one of those groupings, Johnny Bench and Ivan Rodriguez.

13. Al Rosen : Cal Ripkin =

   c. Larry Brown : Walter Payton.

   Larry Brown did not play football nearly as long as Walter Payton, but Brown performed comparably to and in a similar style as Payton—just as Al Rosen did in a similar comparison with Cal Ripkin.

14. Benny Friedman : Dan Marino =

   c. Roger Maris : Reggie Jackson.

   Had Roger Maris not lost a bone in his hand from a sliding accident just two years removed from breaking Babe Ruth's single-season home run record and the speed in his swing as a result, he, too, could have compiled enough longevity-based statistics to gain entrance into the Hall of Fame. Maris was an even better player than Reggie Jackson and also belongs in the Hall of Fame. So, too, does Benny Friedman. He was the most prolific passer of his era and, considering the way the game was played then, just as great a passer as would later be Dan Marino.

15. Hank Greenberg : Lou Gehrig =

   c. Wilt Chamberlain : Bill Russell.

   Only the grouping of Wilt Chamberlain and Bill Russell reflect the level of greatness achieved by both Hank Greenberg and Lou Gehrig.

Mark next to the item that identifies the Gentile athletes.

16. c. Bjorn Borg

17. c. Joe Theisman

18. c. Billy Martin

19. c. Leo Durocher

20. c. Sugar Ray Leonard

Since c is the correct answer for every question, multiplying the number of c answers by five reflects the overall test score from the twenty questions. No particular score has a meaningful implication that can be inferred beyond one's appreciation of Jews in sports.

95–100: Reflects superior sports expertise and analytical skills, or a flaw in the test.

90–100: Reflects appreciation of the top Jews in sports history, or that flaw again.

80–85: Reflects an ability to comprehend ethnic sporting differentials, or the flaw.

70–75: Reflects comprehension that there indeed was more than one.

65 or less: Reflects that "flaw" in the test.

Epilogue

If Howard Cosell really was right in treating sports like a portrayal of life, professional wrestling deserves mention in this book. After all, one of the most popular wrestlers performs under his own Jewish name. Before his star billing in that mode of entertainment, Bill Goldberg had a forgettable three-year run in professional football as a nose guard with the Atlanta Falcons and Los Angeles Rams.

Goldberg made a visit to Capitol Hill memorable by denouncing cock and dog fighting in a highly publicized appearance there. "Animals don't have a choice," he explained to *USA Today*. In a December 1999 *Washington Post* article by Paul Farhi, Goldberg was quoted saying that one of his intentions in becoming a wrestler was to "be a role model to Jewish kids."

And that brings me to a "kid" in Buffalo, who wrote me that my *Jewish Athletes' Hall of Fame* was "terrible" when it came out in 1989. The kid based that opinion on my lack of any mention of a Jewish jockey or horse trainer. I would have liked to explain then that the exclusion of a jockey or horse trainer was intentional, as it is now; that more than two thousand injured horses are euthanized each year.

By now, the kid has grown up. If the grown-up kid writes again, at least I can say that I did mention professional wrestling.

Index

Abarbanel, Mickey, 145
Alcott, Amy, xi, 1, 15, 62–63
Alzado, Lyle, 16, 65–66
Arnovich, Morrie, 17, 120; 141
Asher, Barry, 17, 112–113
Attell, Abe, 1, 4, 16, 66, 141, 167
Ausmus, Brad 17, 130

Baer, Max, 3, 16, 92, 141, 168
Barron, Herman, 145
Barton, Harris, 1, 4, 15, 57–58, 170
Beckham, David, 2–3
Belinsky, Bo, 17, 122–123, 170
Berg, Moe, 143–144, 168–169
Berger, Issac, 4, 16, 77
Berger, Jay, 16, 100–101
Bernstein, Kenny, 16, 78
Blomberg, Ron, 17, 121
Boudreau, Lou, 2, 15, 53–54; 141
Brodsky, Peter, 164
Brooks, Ross, 17, 134–135, 145
Burgin, Elise, 16, 99–100
Buxton, Angela, 2

Clear, Mark, 17, 104–105
Cogan, Tony, 145
Cohan, Donald, 17, 126–127

Cohen, Andy, 17, 128–129, 141, 168
Cohen, Robert, 2

Danning, Harry, 16, 80–81, 141, 169

Edelman, Brad, 17, 106
Epstein, Mike, xi, 17, 111, 170

Fiedler, Jay, 4, 16, 89–91, 171
Fields, Jackie, 16, 71, 141, 168
Fleckman, Marty, 145
Frank, John, 17, 118
Fried, Jeff, 146
Friedman, Benny, 4, 15, 51–52, 141, 168

Gaylord, Mitch, 17, 112
Gilbert, Brad, 16, 95–96
Ginsberg, Joe, 144
Glauber, Keith, 145
Goldberg, Bill, 181
Goldberg, Marshall 15, 60–61, 141, 169
Gordon, Lou, 16, 91–92, 141
Gordon, Sid, 16, 81–82, 141, 169
Gottfried, Brian, 16, 94–95

Green, Shawn, xi, 1, 4, 15, 39–41,
   147, 170, 171
Greenberg, Hank, 1, 8–9, 14, 15,
   19–26, 141, 143, 167, 169
Greenberg, Stephen, 14, 24, 25,
   163
Grossman, Randy, 16, 79
Grunfeld, Ernie, 17, 124–125

Halimi, Alphonse, 2, 3
Handler, Phil, 145
Hartman, Mike, 17, 117–118
Heldman, Julie, 16, 96–97
Helfand, Eric, 144
Henkin, Josh, 146, 147
Hertzberg, Sonny, 16, 103–104,
   141
Heyman, Art, 16, 88–89, 170
Holman, Marshall, 17, 113–114
Holman, Nat, 15, 55–57, 141,
   167–168
Holtzman, Ken, 1, 4, 15, 43–49,
   169, 170

Jaite, Martin, 2

Kaplan, Louis "Kid," 16, 71, 141,
   168
Kapler, Gabe, 4, 17, 108–109
Kitt, Howie, 145
Koufax, Sandy, 1, 3, 13, 15, 26–31,
   143, 170
Kramer, Joel, 17, 134
Krickstein, Aaron, 16, 97–98

LaRusso, Rudy, 16, 71–73
Latman, Barry, 17, 116–117
Leibowitz, David, 160, 161
Leonard, Benny, xi, 1, 11, 15,
   41–42, 141, 167–168
Levine, Al, 17, 132

Levinsky, Battling, 15, 58, 141, 167
Levis, Jesse, 144
Lewis, Ted "Kid," 2, 15, 61, 141,
   167
Lieberman, Nancy, 2, 16, 68–70
Lieberthal, Mike, 3
Lorraine, Andrew, 145
Luckman, Sid, 1, 5, 12–13, 15,
   31–35, 141, 169

Maddox, Elliott, 17, 120
Mansdorf, Amos, 2
Marquis, Jason, 4, 17, 107–108
Martin, Sylvia, 147
Mayer, Erskine, 16, 84–85, 141,
   167
Mesner, Bruce, 17, 133
Messing, Shep, 17, 122
Miller, Norm, 145
Mix, Ron, ix, 9, 15, 37–39, 170
Mondschein, Irv, 145–146
Myer, Buddy, 4, 15, 54–55, 141,
   143, 168

Newhan, David, 144
Newman, Ed, 16, 73–74
Newman, Harry, 4, 16, 68, 161,
   168
Novoselsky, Brent, 17, 127–128

Okker, Tom, 3, 16, 101

Palmer, Jim, 3
Pavin, Corey, 2, 15, 63–64, 171

Radinsky, Scott, 17, 131
Ramenofsky, Marilyn, 5, 17,
   114–116
Revson, Peter, 3, 17, 137–138
Roseanu, Angelica, 2
Rosen, Al, 15, 58–60, 161, 169

Rosen, Goody, 16, 103
Rosenbloom, Maxie, 15, 64, 141, 168
Rosenbluth, Lenny, 17, 105
Ross, Barney, 4, 15, 55, 141, 168
Rossman, Mike, 2, 17, 109–110, 170
Roth, Mark, 16, 83–84

Savitt, Dick, 4, 15, 49–51, 141, 169
Schacht, Al, 143, 144
Schayes, Danny, 17, 130–131
Schayes, Dolph, 1, 10, 15, 36–37, 163, 169
Scheckter, Jody, 2, 3
Scheinblum, Richie, 17, 106–107, 170
Schneider, Mathieu, xi, 4, 16, 80
Schoeneweis, Scott, 4, 17, 123–124
Schwartz, Albert, 17, 125, 141
Shamsky, Art, 17, 119–120, 170
Sherry, Larry, 16, 101–102, 170
Sherry, Norm, 144
Sills, Tony, 145
Silverman, Al, v, 22

Simon, Todd, 145
Solomon, Harold, 16, 92–93
Sper, Jr., Norman, 146
Spitz, Mark, 5, 16, 74–77
Stern, Ronnie, 17, 132
Stone, Steve, 16, 86–88, 170

Tannen, Steve, 16, 93–94
Tauber, Arthur, 146
Teltscher, Eliot, 16, 98–99
Tendler, Lew, 16, 86, 141

Veingrad, Alan, 17, 136–137
Veisor, Mike, 145

Walk, Neal, 16, 85, 86
Weintraub, Paul, 17, 119, 141
Wetzel, Eadie, 147
Wittenberg, Henry, 16, 82–83, 141
Wolfe, Bernie, 145

Young, Roby, 17, 110–111

Zaslofsky, Max, 4, 16, 66–67, 141, 169
Zodsky, Eddy, 144–145

About the Author

B. P. **Robert Stephen Silverman** has been the subject of feature articles in *Government Executive* during his ongoing run through senior positions in nine federal agencies. He has received a commendation from the Comptroller General of the United States for introducing a model for program oversight, the Secretary of the Treasury Honor Award after a widely publicized study he had initiated received major news coverage, an award from the United States Office of Personnel Management for a government-wide innovation, and an award from the Secretary of State. He published the M.A. thesis he completed at the Kent State University School of Journalism about the aftermath of the shooting tragedy there in *College & University Journal* and the dissertation for his Ph.D. from The American University in *Public Relations Review*. While moonlighting for nearly a decade as an adjunct graduate school professor, he published more than forty articles in such scholarly journals as *Business Horizons, Journal of Business Communication, Optimum, Personnel Journal, Public Relations Review, College & University Journal, Compensation Review, Review of Public Personnel Administration,* and *Journal of Systems Management.* He has been cited in textbooks and made many appearances on his "Optimum Legibility Formula," a method for editing precision out of bureaucratic writing; and "The Equal Employment Opportunity Philosophy Index," a neutral four-quadrant model for categorizing differing perceptions on affirmative action of managers and managerial candidates. His exposé in *Personnel Journal,* "Why the Merit Pay System Failed in the Federal Government," resulted in that program's abolishment. He is author of the books *The Jewish Athletes' Hall of Fame* (1989) and *Defending Animals' Rights Is the Right Thing to Do*. The one-time 148-pound DCAAU gold medalist in weight lifting still maintains his high school weight and works out.